WHERE THE LIGHT BREAKS THROUGH

A LEADER'S STORY OF LOVE, LOSS, LEARNING, AND A FIERCE RETURN TO THE LIGHT

AMY MEREDITH

InvisibleInk

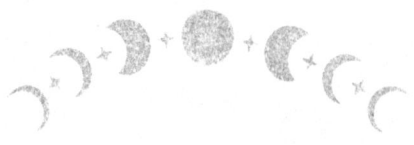

This book is dedicated to each version of me who kept going—
without a map, a manual, or permission.
You were always worthy.
I've got us now.

No longer lend your strength
to that which you wish to be free from.

Fill your lives with love and bravery
and you shall lead a life uncommon.

—Jewel Kilcher, "Life Uncommon," Spirit (1998)

A NOTE TO THE READER

I've done my best to tell these stories with honesty, care, and respect for everyone included. I recognize there will always be different perspectives. This is simply my telling—my lived experience—shared with the intention to harm no one, but to vulnerably offer the hard truths so many of us navigate in silence.

This book holds pieces of my story that are tender and, at times, heavy. Some chapters include experiences of trauma. You'll read about a childhood navigating adult situations like smoking, drinking, and exposure to pornography, as well as instances of inappropriate touching between middle schoolers, sexual assault in high school, a car accident, several instances of sudden illness, deep heartbreak and personal loss.

These memories aren't shared lightly. I've included them not for shock, but for truth, and for all of us who've carried more than our share at too young an age. While they may bring up painful memories or emotions, my hope is they will help you feel less alone.

Please take care of yourself as you read. It's okay to take breaks. It's okay to skip ahead. Your well-being matters most.

At the end of the book, you'll find a list of resources. If anything stirs something in you—or you find yourself needing a little extra care—I hope you'll reach for support.

You are not alone. You never were.

With tenderness and truth,
Amy

INTRODUCTION
IDLE TUESDAYS

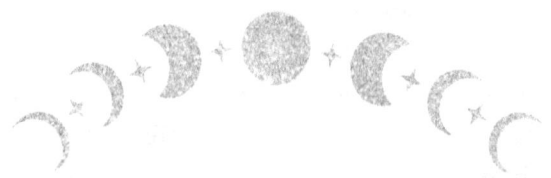

It's never the dramatic days that undo you. It's the quiet ones—the Tuesdays that start with coffee and end with a phone call that splits your life in two.

It's those moments. Those turning points. The ones where suddenly there's a before and an after.

If we're lucky, we each only get a few of those.

Sometimes, I feel like I've had more than my share.

Although I know so many people have carried far more, when they start to stack up, they can feel like more than we can bear. That's when you really feel their weight.

For me, it clings to the back of my throat like a knot that keeps me from using my voice—quite literally, like someone's foot is on my throat, pressing down, holding me in place.

It was an idle Tuesday in early April when two young 13-year-olds took the car for a joyride up to the *Country Pantry* to grab some smokes—planning to be back before the babies even woke up.

It was an idle Tuesday when I learned my parents were getting divorced.

It was an idle Tuesday when my grandmother called to tell me my mother's cancer was back.

We thought we had beaten it. We thought we were in the clear. But everything came crashing down again with that one phone call. I was just beginning to exhale. To make plans again. To believe in healing. And then—just like that—we were right back in the storm.

It was an idle Tuesday when we found out the bank had called TW's note. Things were going to change. Dramatically. Forever.

It was an idle Tuesday when my sister, just 8 years old, called and asked, in her most innocent voice, if I thought our mom was going to make it through the night. Little did she know, it would be her very last.

I barely remember getting the call that my dad was in the hospital. He had called 911 himself. It wasn't looking good—an aortic dissection—and they were prepping him for emergency surgery.

It was an idle Tuesday when my Uncle David called and said the words out loud: "Your dad is gone." There's no gentle way to say it, and he didn't have it in him to try.

Just the truth. Sudden. Irreversible.
    I can still hear the quiet in his voice.

It was another Tuesday when the EMS driver called me. Matt had been in a car accident. The details came through in pieces—glass, headlights, sirens—but the sound of the phone ringing is what still echoes.

I didn't realize the severity until I arrived in the ER.

Most of Matt's seizures have come on idle weekdays too—quiet mornings or ordinary afternoons, between 7am and 10pm. The slow fade, the lost time, the scrambling afterward.

My nervous system had learned to watch those days the way some people watch the sky for storms. You never know which ones will turn.

And it was an idle Tuesday when the break-in happened.

Just after the anniversary of my mother's death.

A glass door shattered. Jewelry gone. Heirlooms lost.

Another ordinary day that ended with that feeling in your stomach—the one that tells you nothing will ever be the same.

No one warns you that grief doesn't wait for a convenient moment.

That it sneaks up on you and takes your very breath away when you least expect it.

It doesn't knock.

It doesn't circle back when you're more ready—and let's face it, we're never ready for all that grief brings.

That's just part of it.

It comes when it comes.

And it knocks you off your feet.

Pulls the rug right out from under you.

And more often than not, it shows up quietly—

on some idle, ordinary day.

These are the moments that shaped me. You'll learn the details soon enough—but first, I want to show you how they felt.

THE ONLY WAY OUT IS THROUGH

IT'S strange how an ordinary day can feel like any other: quiet, new, and full of small routines. Right up until the moment everything shifts.

It's a cold December morning. The sky is still dark as I warm pasta for the kids' thermoses. My children, Olivia and Parker, attend a small Montessori school without a cafeteria, so we pack lunches daily. They've gotten themselves dressed and are eating breakfast when I hear it — that distinct sound my husband makes when a seizure begins.

Like Pavlov's bell, it has conditioned me. My body reacts before my mind does. It's a warning bell, the moment I hear it, the world stops. I drop everything and run to him. If I'm fast enough, I reach him before his body slams into the floor, wall, or whatever piece of furniture is in his path.

On the best days, I catch him in time, lower him gently to the floor, and shield his head from injury.

My nervous system jolts, then freezes. But I don't have the luxury of staying frozen. My priorities are clear: take care of him, care for our children. So I move.

This morning, I caught him and helped him to the floor. It's a waiting game now.

He looks like he's dying. His skin turns bluish as his body convulses. His eyes are open, but he's not there. I cradle his head in my hands. Parker hovers, worried. I ask him to bring us a pillow and tell him I love him. I soften my voice, so it's steady enough to hold him too. I tell him he's brave, that I know this is hard to watch, that it will be over soon... we wait.

I time it. I watch for breath. His body jerks, his eyes roll back, and fear presses into my throat. It's excruciating to witness. But like so many things in life, the only way out is through.

Parker slips the pillow under his father's head, then nestles into my left side while Matt lies to my right. We wait. Parker is five. Olivia stays across the room — distance is how she protects herself. She is seven. I call to her gently, remind her that I love her, that Daddy will be okay, that this will pass.

And then, it begins to slow.

The convulsing stops. The gasping begins, his lungs fighting to refill with oxygen that he has struggled to take in for the last minutes that feel like a lifetime. Parker gets a cold washcloth and a towel. Matt is drenched in sweat, but safe. This time, we were lucky. I caught him before he fell. No head injury. We did everything right. Still—it never feels like enough.

He comes back slowly. Then his eyes scan the room, wide and uncertain. Those first moments, he often looks panicked, in his body present but his mind still catching up. He doesn't remember any of it. His truth will become what I tell him happened.

Parker brings the washcloth, and I gently wipe his face, trying to meet him with calm and warmth.

I wait for him to look at me.

"Hi," he says, a soft smile. Every time.

He kisses me, tells me he loves me.

And every time, I feel grateful for that. For the way he loves me. For his softness, even here.

"I love you," I say back. "You had a seizure. You're okay. You're safe."

Parker hugs him and tells him he loves him.

I ask a few gentle questions to see if he's coming to the way he normally does.

We follow our standard protocol—recovery can take anywhere from twenty to forty-five minutes. We are in the postictal state now. The National Library of Medicine says most seizures aren't dangerous and typically pass within minutes, but my nervous system doesn't get the memo.

We use an app called "Self Help for Trauma." It walks us through a tapping sequence that helps our bodies come back to center. It doesn't erase what just happened, but it gives us something to do. A path through the aftermath. A reset button if you will.

The Tapping Solution Foundation says, "Tapping gives you the power to heal yourself, putting the control over your destiny back into your own hands." That's exactly what it feels like. It doesn't take away the fear or the helplessness, but it gives us a way to process it. To release some of the charge. To keep going.

Olivia keeps her distance. I remind her that protecting her own peace is something she never had to apologize for. I want her to feel empowered by that choice. As the adult, it's my job to help Dad and keep everyone safe. Her job is to take care of herself, and that's more than enough. The adults in the room are managing the crisis. This isn't hers to carry.

Parker, on the other hand, wants to help. I thank him and remind him that he already has helped. I tell him it's okay to feel whatever he feels, whether that's fear, confusion, or something else entirely. Even if they are conflicting, both can be true. I always return to this: there is no wrong way to respond. No shame. Their job is to care for themselves in a way that feels safe and manageable.

Once Matt is resting, I shift back into mom mode. I reassure the kids. I tend to their emotional needs first because even if they seem to bounce back quicker than I do, I know these moments live deep inside them. As Bessel van der Kolk wrote in "The Body Keeps the Score."

Thankfully, this time, there's no physical injury. I help him to bed, bring him water, ibuprofen, and the missed a dose of medication I find on the counter — frustrated but relieved to have a reason. He calls work to take the day off.

Matt has generalized idiopathic epilepsy — a condition often diagnosed in childhood that, in plain terms, is a fancy way of saying "we don't know what causes the seizures." While some people eventually "grow out" of this type of epilepsy, Matt hasn't, which makes it harder to treat. Still, we hold onto hope. One of his uncles stopped having seizures in his forties, and that's been our quiet wish for Matt, too.

Then I return to the rhythm of our morning. No one's really up for breakfast, and I don't push them. I answer their questions. I hold space.

We move slowly. We tap.

Because when you've watched someone you love look like they might be dying, your breath doesn't come back right away.

We begin the slow process of resetting for the day ahead. We gather our belongings: backpacks, lunches, winter layers, my work bag. We load the car.

On the way to school, I ask what they'd like for dinner, what they'd most love to do that night. I tell them we'll do it, no matter what. I'm grateful because it's usually something so doable: grilled cheese or Mexican food, maybe a cozy show with extra cuddles. "*Yes, please.*" These simple rituals help me too. They give us something to look forward to.

At drop-off, I hug them longer than usual. I remind them I can't wait to see them after school. Once they've gone to their classrooms, I let the front desk know —lightly—that the kids might need a little extra grace, hugs, and understanding. No details. They don't need them. They understand, and they respond with compassion. I'm grateful. I breathe a small sigh of relief.

Back in the parking lot, I pause to catch my breath and send their teachers a quick heads-up email so they know what the kids are walking in with. I let the quiet wrap around me before I race into the next thing.

I'm already late. And I'm headed toward a job I've grown to hate.

I brace myself. The manager I report to, doesn't seem to have much experience as a leader. In my experience, it was a very male dominated environment with long lunches for management, cubicles for the rest of us.

These are the hardest days, the ones that start with a seizure, and still expect you to do the rest of your life. They're depleting. Exhausting. All-consuming.

I pep talk myself through the day ahead. I separate the must-do's: the ones for me, the ones for Matt, the ones for our kids. I am his person, and he needs support in these recovery windows. The children need support. Our household needs my income. The pets, the meals, the homework, the invisible work of holding it all together—it all stacks up until I can barely remember the version of myself that came before this.

I keep wishing it could all be simpler. But the truth is, it's anything but.

And all this caretaking—today, every day—takes me back. To my childhood. To my twenties. To a lifetime of learning how to hold it all, even when it feels like too much.

IN THE SHADOWS

As I drive to work in a dissociated state, I replay the morning in my mind. The hours following a seizure hit me hard—cortisol surging, my body on edge. Recovery for Matt is shorter now, but in those first few moments, I'm back in patterns of my childhood: my needs on hold, scanning the environment for safety, bracing for what comes next.

On seizure days, our lives are transformed in an instant. How we spend the rest of the day depends on the severity, the damage, the aftermath, and how many hours we have until we can reasonably end the day. My first job is protecting Matt physically. My second is holding space for the emotional well-being of our kids—for Matt too. Everyone's nervous systems are on high alert, looking to me for safety and regulation.

Before his surgery in 2015, recovery from seizures was longer, harder, and more unpredictable. The implant he received that year— a small device in his chest that sends pulses to the vagus nerve— changed that. Now, when a seizure starts, I swipe a magnet over it, and more often than not, it cuts the episode short and softens the crash that follows. It's been a gift, not just for his body, but for our whole family. For the first time, we had a tool to respond with, leaving us feeling less helpless and him feeling less drained.

That first year with the implant began after a terrifying day—Matt had a seizure while driving to work, totaling our SUV. I'll never forget answering the phone to an EMT explaining they were taking him to University Hospital. I didn't understand the severity at the time. He walked away with only minor injuries, but the what-ifs stayed with me.

Even with the device, seizure days still drain me. I move through on autopilot, checking boxes to keep everyone safe and fed. Dinners are simple, unless a friend or family member brings something over. By nightfall, I am completely tapped out.

It brings me back to my mother's cancer, and all we could do was sit beside her as it had its way with her. Or to those weeks after my father's aortic dissection, when he lay in a medically induced coma, when he finally woke, he asked for my mother, who had been gone more than a year.

By the time I turn onto the street I work on, I am back in the present. There's no capacity left for extra demands or drama. I am in survival mode. I have surrendered all empathy for the day for my loved ones. My cup is empty and it's not even 10:00 am.

Crisis management was nothing new to me—it just looked different in the office than it did at home.

My grandfather, TW they called him, built his import and manufacturing business from the ground up. My great-grandmother —his mother-in-law—was an investor. She had carefully saved her wages while working during World War II. I always loved that detail. What a union. She was a gem in her own right.

Over four decades, TW grew the company into a respected opera-tion. He was kind, humble, and generous—a leader who genuinely cared about people. He was so down to Earth. But like many leaders, he had a blind spot: he struggled to have the hard conversations. He avoided conflict and didn't always hold people accountable.

When poor performance or toxic behavior goes unchecked—especially in a family-run business—cracks form. Some people begin to take advantage. Inventory started disappearing. One item became two, then it snowballed. Loans went unpaid. Eventually, multiple people were helping themselves.

The scale of the business made it hard to detect at first. But once word spread and others joined in, the ripple effects grew. By the time the numbers stopped lining up and the bank called his note, it was too late. Over a million dollars in unpaid customer orders. The empire was crumbling.

I was brought in around the time of Hurricane Katrina and the days leading to the 2008 recession. At first it was a unique opportunity to learn from him, then to help identify the problem areas and bring accountability.

I had long admired my grandfather's legacy. With a passion for understanding human behavior, my psychology degree gave me the theory, but real life taught me that people, with all their power struggles and blind spots, are the hardest part of any business. TW's deep loyalty was one of his greatest strengths. A true Leo—confident, generous, charismatic, with a big ole heart—he sometimes avoided holding accountable those who were taking advantage of the company's inventory and resources. Navigating those dynamics requires skill, structure, and often outside support. Some issues TW wanted me to address; others he asked me not to. I told him that was a problem.

"People are the hardest part of business," he'd say. "People are strange." And he was right.

In some ways, TW was still running his multimillion dollar business like a mom and pop shop, trusting in handshake deals and face-to-face integrity. But the business had grown—tens of thousands of feet of warehouse space after multiple additions, plus thousands more in the factory and the pipe yard. The stakes were higher. Everyone had bills to pay.

It couldn't last forever. The cracks were already there—customer slow pay, no pay and disappearing inventory, the quiet shifts in loyalty that you can feel before you can prove. Eventually, we sat in a meeting at the bank and staring down the truth: we needed to find a buyer. Several individuals stepped up. The bulk of the funding came from Chinese investors, connected through one of his longtime business partners. They brought factory backers and swept in to take the problem off his hands. It was bittersweet. Heartbreaking. Excruciating to watch.

Leadership is complex. People are complicated. And the hardest part of any business—the part that can make or break it—is always human.

And then, one day—midway through the wind-down process—my grandfather just stopped coming to the office. I don't think he even realized it was his last day. I think his soul had reached its limit and could no longer bear the torturous process of losing everything he spent more than half of his life building. The weight of watching everything he built disappear was too heavy to bear. I didn't blame him. I couldn't imagine what it must have felt like.

That left me at the top working with finance, consultants, longtime vendors and clients. I was 33 years old, leading the wind-down team, working directly with the acquiring company. I was also a mom with a newborn, a 2-year-old, and a 16-year-old, since my sister was living with us at that point.

Looking back, my background in psychology helped me see what was happening beneath the surface, not just for my grandfather, but for others who had quietly built their lives around the business too. There was fear. Grief. Uncertainty. And powerlessness doesn't always look like panic; it often hides behind polite smiles, missed deadlines, and poor performance reviews that try to say something without really saying it.

Resilience doesn't always look like strength. Sometimes it looks like showing up for the next right thing, even when you're scared and feeling broken, with a newborn in one arm and a crumbling business in the other.

KICK ME WHEN I'M DOWN

As I walked in late on that cold December morning, I was greeted by my boss. He wasn't supposed to be onsite, so I immediately knew something was wrong. *What is he doing here?* I don't have the energy for any more surprises today.

He called me into the conference room.

"We're letting you go," he said. "We're outsourcing your work."

I sat there, blindsided, just staring back at him. My mind flashed to a conversation we'd had several months earlier, when I'd told them I needed to scale back my hours. I was tired of fighting traffic just to be the last parent picking up my kids from aftercare. It wasn't working anymore. I needed more time with my children. I'd given them a plan that I thought worked for everyone. Sitting there that morning, I realized that change may have also made it easier for them to make this decision.

Because of TW's lifelong dedication and hard work, the new owners now had inherited a thriving business. Letting me go felt like being tossed out with the bath water.

They offered me a severance package and asked me to sign right then and there. All I could think of were the years I'd spent sitting beside my grandfather while we signed documents. *Sign here. Initial there. Date this line.*

Only now, my brain couldn't even comprehend what was happening. I was still frozen, stuck in the trauma of the moment, of the morning I'd had. So I signed it, took the severance, and was handed a box to start packing up my things.

My things from more than a decade working in the building my grandfather had purchased nearly 25 years earlier. There was so much history. So many memories. So many laughs I'd shared with him there. So much time, treasured time, I'd spent in that space. And it was all coming to an end without warning. It took my breath away.

They didn't allow me to say my goodbyes—a standard business practice in termination, but still a gut punch after so many years. These were people I'd worked alongside for years, some since the late nineties when I first started working after school.

By this point, I too had spent more than half of my life connected to this business in one way or another.

I was blindsided. Humiliated. Heartbroken.

At that moment, I felt shattered and like a failure. I took my items to the car and headed home in shock.

I had no idea that this heartbreak—as painful as it was—would eventually shape the way I built teams and culture in my own work. I came to understand firsthand what it felt like to me to be unseen, unheard, and dismissed, and I knew I wanted to lead differently.

2

SMOKE 'EM IF YOU'VE GOT 'EM

I ATTENDED PUBLIC GRADE SCHOOL. Private school wasn't in our budget and honestly, I'm not sure it was even on my parents' radar. It just wasn't an option for us.

From an early age, I felt othered. Most of the kids on our street went to Catholic school. They always seemed to have half-days and extra time off. Except for my friends, the twins, nearly everyone my age in the neighborhood wore uniforms and went somewhere I didn't.

In second grade, my teacher recommended I be tested for giftedness. By third grade, I was moved into the advanced program, which meant changing schools. When my friends came knocking to play, I was stuck inside with what felt like hours of homework each night. It was hard. I felt restricted. Left out. I wanted to be outside roaming the neighborhood with them, but I had to finish my assignments first. That shift started creating even more distance between me and the two closest friends I had.

At some point in the third grade, my babysitter, Mindy started giving me cigarettes. I was eight. She would share them with me after school, encourage me to have another and laugh hysterically as I choked on the poisonous smoke. This was probably one of the first examples of when the wrong attention took me down a darker path. The older I got, the more I realized how *off* she was. Mindy was 16 and in Catholic school; her family lived up the street from us. She would come over to "watch us" in the summer and sometimes after school.

Her dad worked at Phillip Morris, like many in our town. As a benefit of working there, employees got to take cigarettes home for free—what a bonus. The Marlboros made their way to us in these cute little packs of five and our top choices were Reds and Lights. There seemed to be an endless supply of them. In those days, I knew several people whose parents worked there and it was common to have a supply of cigarettes in their homes that could have stocked a local convenience store. It was hard for the adults to even realize any were missing.

Mindy would always bring extra Marlboros with her and give some to me. She must have thought it was hilarious to watch an eight-year-old smoke them because she had no problem giving them to me, what a joke. I'd inhale and nearly cough up a lung as my young body resisted while she cracked up watching me.

I got better at it though and learned to cough less. I thought I was cool. At the time, I was not the only kid in grade school smoking, I had another friend up the street that I smoked with, Lisa. However, I do think I was the only kid in my Brownie troop who smoked. Don't worry, I didn't smoke at Brownies, I hid it from most kids. I do remember waiting on the porch in my little khaki-colored uniform once, smoking a cigarette waiting for my ride to Girl Scouts. I don't think I was the poster child for their mission.

My new elementary school was next door to the local high school, separated only by a small field. We were close enough to see when the high schoolers were out and what they were up to. We would be outside for recess playing ball and getting bullied. Then we would see all of the high schoolers outside between classes, smoking cigarettes in the parking lot. It was no big deal, it was the 80s, and that's how things were. By the time I reached middle school, I knew a lot of kids who smoked.

QUEENS OF THE CUL-DE-SAC

Sometimes on the weekends I'd spend the night with my maternal grandmother, Nanny. She'd been in a wheelchair since I was five, after a car accident that left her paralyzed from the waist down. She spent weeks in the hospital, where she learned that she would never walk or dance again. She had to relearn how to use her arms and hands for even the most basic tasks: feeding herself, writing her name. She used wide-handled silverware to maintain her grip and often needed help cutting her food. Writing was especially hard, holding and controlling a pen was difficult.

It was an unimaginable transition for someone so vibrant and full of life, and yet, she never let on. I never saw anything less than a radiant, light-hearted angel who made me feel like I was her greatest joy. She showered everyone around her with love, grace, and quiet wisdom. Her voice was gentle, her smile glowing, her laugh unforgettable. Somehow, after all she'd endured, she remained luminous.

After the accident, she and my grandfather divorced. A relative later told me she'd made the decision herself, not because he would've left, but because she knew the accident had changed everything. So she started over. She had a replica of their farmhouse built in a new neighborhood, complete with an elevator. As kids, we thought that was the coolest thing in the world. I can't even count how many times we rode that elevator from the second floor to the basement. We were certain we were royalty.

I loved staying the night with her. In the mornings, we'd lie in her big bed with breakfast trays, watching TV, talking, and just being together. It was our special one-on-one time, and she never missed an opportunity to tell me how loved I was. I soaked up every second.

On the days she felt well enough, she'd get ready and come downstairs. On harder days, she stayed in bed. She had live-in care-takers to assist with bathing, dressing, cooking, and cleaning, two spare bedrooms were always ready for rotating support. Being the polished woman she was, they also helped her apply her makeup. People used to say she and my mom were the best-dressed women they knew. Impeccable taste. Fabulous laughs. Wise words. Beautiful eyes. And always lipstick in the photos. As a young child who didn't like to make a fuss, I didn't always get it. But now, missing the matri-archs of my family, I'm starting to understand—and even channel—a little more of their grace and charm into my own style. And you can absolutely find me reaching for a lipstick before a good photo.

If I asked her caregivers if they would do my makeup too, they almost always lovingly agreed. It was another highlight of those visits—someone doting over me, making me feel special and grown up.

We were a duo. And on her good days, she'd ask the same ques-tion: "Want to go for a walk?"

Of course, I always said yes.

Sometimes I'd walk beside her, sometimes I'd ride in her lap as she steered us both down the street in her motorized wheelchair. We'd cruise to the end of the road and back. We were queens of the cul-de-sac. I loved the wind in my hair, the feeling of her arms around me, the unbroken attention of someone who loved me deeply and fully. On special days, we'd even venture even further, off on some great suburban adventure.

Holidays at Nanny's were their own kind of magic—festive decorations, intricate table settings, amazing food, and unlimited cans of caffeine-free Coke and Sprite for the grandkids. We were in heaven. The only downside was how many places we had to go in one day. Just as we'd settle in, it would be time to pack up and head to another relative's house. But I treasured every moment.

HURT PEOPLE HURT PEOPLE

I closed out fifth grade by getting in trouble at school. It was the first time something like that happened. This was one of the early moments igniting my decades-long relationship with shame. I bullied a classmate after being bullied, too. I made fun of a boy and passed around a paper that said something mean about him for classmates to see. Even worse, I asked them all to sign it. Possibly some early tendencies toward advocacy, channeled in the wrong direction. It was extremely hurtful to the boy and I felt so much shame around it for years. Now I understand that I was in pain and it was a cry for help, but no one recognized that at the time.

Instead, I apologized to him and was no longer allowed to participate in the week-long class trip to Pine Mountain with my classmates. Ostracized from something we had all been looking forward to, this left me feeling alone again. I had already been to Pine Mountain once before and had been looking forward to it. Now I knew what I would be missing. Saddened, that shame got even heavier. I'd hurt someone, disappointed my teacher, my parents and myself. I didn't even really know why I had done it. It was one of those things someone else started and I took it and ran with it. Only I took it too far.

Looking back from the perspective of an adult and a parent, I know going on that trip would have been so good for me. Spending a week in nature, being social with my classmates would have been a beneficial experience for me to connect with my peers, instead I felt left behind. I was ten. That was one of the first times I remember feeling really excluded. I got labeled a "bad kid" and the rest of fifth grade was tough and grew even more lonely.

I began increasingly feeling the need to escape. I spent my middle school days fascinated by my dad's collection of "Omni" magazines. I went through many of them in those hours after school. As a latchkey kid, I filled my afternoons rummaging through the basement or the attic for something to do or having my friends over. We would usually end up getting into my dad's record collection and blasting our favorite tunes on the Cerwin Vega speakers in our living room that stood nearly as tall as me. We sang loudly, danced and laughed, it was always so much fun.

We rotated Don Henley's "All She Wants to Do Is Dance," Madonna's "Like a Virgin" album, The Beatles "Sgt. Pepper's Lonely Hearts Club Band," Michael Jackson "Thriller" and more. Music was such an influential piece of my life, expression, and experience. In middle school, I started writing more regularly. From poems to journals to song lyrics, notebooks, folders, and pieces of paper, I loved to write. I found it very healing and helpful in my processing. I felt better when I put things on paper and out of my body. I sometimes curiously wonder how things would have gone had I connected with more creatives and spent more time making things, hanging out in libraries and bookstores. Instead, I was smoking and drinking but it was all part of my journey that brought me to where I am now.

"JUST SAY NO" AND OTHER CHILDHOOD NIGHTMARES

Aside from the usual childhood worries, there was a whole laundry list of ways to die in the 80s, starting with the ever-present fear of razor blades in our Halloween candy, and stretching all the way to drowning if we didn't wait a full thirty minutes after eating before swimming. We were told that one rogue bite of a sandwich followed by a cannonball could end it all.

Between the *Just Say No* campaign, terrifying after school specials, and slasher films like "Texas Chainsaw Massacre" and "Nightmare on Elm Street," the message was clear: danger lurked everywhere. You could be abducted from the grocery store, stuck by lightning (nowhere seemed safe) or vanish into the Bermuda Triangle. We lacked the constant technology of today, but somehow we were still certain our lives could end at any moment.

Eighties kids had a spectacularly dramatic list of things to fear, thanks to a perfect storm of 24-hour news, sensational PSAs, and parents who were raised on "Unsolved Mysteries" and "Dateline." Add in the moral panic around satanic cults, the ever-looming threat of "Stranger Danger," quicksand (which we assumed was a very real and frequent threat), abandoned wells, nuclear war, and the faces of

missing kids staring at us from milk cartons and you've got a generation of kids whose sense of safety was always a little shaky.

It seemed like every day there was something new to avoid or
else risk certain doom. My mom had a friend who was abducted and
murdered in high school—by a motorcycle gang, as she told it—so
we were especially terrified of any group of men on motorcycles.
How could you tell if they were a gang? I just learned to stay away.

And yet for all that fear-based education, no one ever explained
the *actual* threats that were close to us. We were warned about
strangers, but no one taught us how to navigate the people we
already knew—the ones who touched us without consent, who said
things that made us uncomfortable, who took liberties with our
space and our silence.

Middle school was a particularly confusing and vulnerable time
for me. Like most other moments of my life, I felt like I didn't fit in. I
was bussed out of my neighborhood to attend the advanced program
at Newburg Middle, which was a big shift from my elementary
school experience. I was suddenly surrounded by more diverse
groups of people and unfamiliar social norms. I rode the school bus
with kids who lived closer to my part of town in Fern Creek, and
somehow I ended up sitting in the back. Looking back now, it almost
certainly would've been better if I'd chosen a different seat.

The back of the bus was filled with a handful of boys who identi-
fied as "hoods"—white, working- and lower-middle-class suburban
bad boy wannabes. There was constant sexual joking, casual touching, and an atmosphere of discomfort I didn't have language for. I
was grabbed inappropriately—my chest, my butt—and I didn't
know how to make it stop. At the time, I didn't even fully realize how
inappropriate it was. In 1989, these weren't things we talked about.

No one had taught me how to use my voice to protect myself
from everyday violations like these. I'm sure my parents lovingly
shared some basic safety rules, probably around strangers. I mean,
my dad taught me how to throw a punch. Just in case I ever needed
to, as a last resort, but nothing that helped me navigate the actual

danger I faced. I think that's part of what kept me an easy target: I didn't know how to name what was happening. I didn't know how to stop it. And I was already carrying a sense of shame I couldn't articulate.

Those weren't isolated incidents on the bus. The same kinds of things happened to me at the mall, the movies, amusement parks— people grabbing my body in ways that left me stunned and unsure how to respond. And because I didn't know how to talk about it—or feared I'd be blamed or accused of "asking for it"—I stayed silent.

Now, looking back, I can see that my then-undiagnosed neurodivergence likely played a role in that silence. I didn't always have the language for what I was feeling, or even the ability to recognize those feelings right away. I often froze, unsure of what to say or how to react, and by the time I could begin to make sense of what had happened, the moment had already passed. It was easier to stay quiet than to stumble through an explanation I didn't fully understand myself.

Maybe I liked the attention. Maybe I didn't know what to say. Maybe I was afraid of making it worse. But more than anything, I think I lacked the internal script that other kids seemed to have— how to name discomfort, how to set a boundary, how to say "no" in a way that stuck. Without that framework, I just absorbed what happened. It stayed quiet, and it stayed mine.

Middle school is disorienting even in the best of circumstances. No one really knows what they're doing. Everyone's awkward, everyone's trying to find their way, and often they get it wrong—at the expense of other kids. I didn't have the tools to stand up for myself or even name what was happening. I wasn't just overwhelmed by the behavior around me—I was paralyzed by my own confusion about how to process it.

And because I didn't talk to anyone about it, I just kept carrying it. Like so many other things, I internalized it without understanding it, filing it under "things I must be doing wrong."

I dreaded the bus. I was one of the first to get on in the morning and one of the last to get off in the afternoon—making for a 45-minute ride each way. The sounds, the smells, the personal violations, the chaos of adolescence, it was all so much. But I stayed in that back seat, every day, even though it never once felt safe.

My brain didn't filter out what was irrelevant—it flagged everything as potentially important. That kind of sensory input doesn't leave much space for fast reactions. It just meant it took longer to untangle. And when the noise and movement and touching all happened at once, I often went quiet inside, disoriented, disconnected.

I'd sit in silence, staring out the window, counting the stops until mine. That became my anchor. I didn't track time by minutes, I tracked it by who got off where. Five stops to go. Then four. Then three. I couldn't always make sense of what was happening around me, but I knew exactly how many stops stood between me and a quieter place. Home wasn't always safe but it usually offered a soft landing, a place to recalibrate at least for a few hours. I'd spend my quiet time replaying events in my head, wishing I could go back and say what I needed to say. Then, the instability of the evening set in.

UNSPOKEN RULES

By seventh grade, there was one girl at school who simply didn't like me. I'm not sure why. I mostly kept to myself and came across as quiet and shy unless you knew me well. But one afternoon on the bus, mid-ride home, she stood up and shouted, "Somebody give me some scissors, I'm gonna cut this bitch's hair off!"

I froze. I was horrified. She was most certainly *not* going to cut my hair off and she wasn't going to get me with those scissors either.

At that moment, I dissociated. I pretty much blacked out. I think it happened quickly. I threw punch after punch to defend myself until she was on the bus floor, and someone pulled me off of her. I was in shock—completely out of my body. Her nose was bleeding, my hands were shaking, my heart was racing. But it was over. And thankfully, we were both mostly okay—physically, anyway.

I went to the principal's office and said it was self-defense. I don't even remember if I got in trouble at school, but I do know I wasn't in trouble at home. My father had always made it clear: I would never be punished for defending myself. I think he was proud I stood my ground.

I never heard another word from her on the bus after that. She sat quietly, looking out the window while the other kids teased her for starting something and getting beat up. But that was never who I wanted to be. I didn't feel triumphant. I felt sorry for her. I didn't like that it had come to that. It felt like a loss... for both of us. Looking back, it was probably one of my first understandings of how hurt people hurt people. And still, I protected myself, because no one else was going to. And after that, no one else gave me much shit either.

A few months earlier, my dad had taught me how to throw a punch. He was a total egalitarian—always teaching that violence was never the answer and that there was usually a better way to resolve things. But he also taught me that just because you didn't start shit didn't mean you had to take it either.

One of the most impactful things he taught me was this: sometimes in life, people will treat you badly, and when they do, you don't have to take it. You pick up your stuff, turn around, and walk away.

But here's the complicated part—because of my then-undiagnosed neurodivergence, I didn't always realize when I was being treated badly. What was blatantly obvious to others wasn't always clear to me. I misread tone, missed social cues, and assumed I was overreacting. So I didn't always walk away. Sometimes I stayed too long. Sometimes I internalized what happened, assuming it was just me.

I think about her sometimes. About how we were both just kids, trying to survive middle school in our own ways, shaped by the worlds we came from. I think about what it must've felt like for her after that day—not just to lose the fight, but to be mocked and isolated afterward. And I wonder what else she was carrying, what was happening in her world that made me her target that day.

I didn't have the language for any of that back then. But even at 12, I knew this wasn't just about me. Something in me recognized the power imbalance, the way she was treated afterward, the way the kids jeered at her. It didn't feel right. And even though I hadn't started it—and was just defending myself—I still carried the weight of it. I could see something in her that I knew in myself: that lonely, left-out feeling, the way silence gets misunderstood and bullied. We were more alike than anyone on that bus probably realized.

My parents had raised me to believe that everyone should be treated equally, no matter their gender, race or background. And at that middle school, surrounded by students from all kinds of backgrounds, I was slowly starting to see how the world didn't always work that way. That moment on the bus was one of the first times I really felt injustice, not just of what happened, but of what it meant. It was a defining moment.

I didn't know it then, but that experience planted the seed of something I'd carry with me for the rest of my life. A fierce sense of justice. A heart for the underdog. An instinct to speak up when someone is being mistreated, even if I didn't yet know how.

That day on the bus, though, something clicked. I didn't want to fight, but I wasn't about to let her hurt me. I didn't know what would happen next, but at least I knew I had options. And for once, I didn't feel frozen in place.

That day didn't make me who I am, but it showed me something I couldn't unsee. About how people get treated. About who gets defended. About who gets left behind.

I can still feel what it felt like to sit on that bus afterward—my hands still shaking, my body coming down, my heart heavy in ways I couldn't explain. I didn't have the language for it, but something shifted in me that day.

And eventually, something shifted between us too. We gradually made our way to speaking terms and called a truce. I don't remember how we got there exactly, but over time, things softened. We were never close, but we found our way back to speaking. Maybe even laughing about it, in that way middle school kids sometimes do when the intensity fades and all that's left is the shared awkwardness of growing up. It wasn't a perfect resolution, but it was real. And it stayed with me.

TRYING TO LOOK LIKE I BELONGED
FRIENDSHIP AT FULL VOLUME

I met one of my oldest friends in seventh grade science class. I ended up sitting next to Jennifer, she introduced herself and then followed up by asking if I had ever kissed a boy. I lied and said yes, as she looked like a girl who most certainly had and would teach me a thing or two about it. Jennifer and I became fast friends. We lived not too far from one another and found our way into all kinds of situations that later terrified me. The first time she invited me over was a weekday after school. She made us margaritas, turned on one of her parent's pornos, and made herself comfortable on the couch like we were watching a soap opera. It was extremely awkward and uncomfortable, at like 4:30, on a random Wednesday afternoon. I had no idea how to respond so I just rolled with it.

By then, I was no stranger to sex. Not because anyone had talked to me about it, but because my babysitter had made sure of that. Aside from smoking, one of Mindy's other pastimes was rummaging through all of my parent's drawers and belongings, then sharing their copy of the "Joy of Sex" book she had found with us. Looking at those penciled-in drawings was weird but much easier to stomach than the porn video. She even used to ask us questions about what we thought about different poses, I mean what the hell? It was pretty twisted, I was in like fourth grade at the time. I sure would have preferred that book to what I was now witnessing on Jennifer's couch, terrified her parents might come home at any minute. She was popular and I wanted to look cool, so I rolled with it.

Not too long after, Jennifer and I started sneaking out. We would meet up in the middle of the night, connect with other neighborhood kids and roam the streets with the thrill of experiencing a whole new world. It channeled my rebellious side and gave me a newfound sense of freedom. I stepped into two of my biggest lifelong identities in middle school: victim and rebel badass.

It was one or the other, or some combination of both, depending on the moment. In middle school, I mimicked and mirrored others constantly. I would later learn this was a neurodivergent trait: adapting by reflecting the behaviors and expressions of those around me. At the time, I didn't have language for it. I just knew I could blend in, shift easily, and connect with people from all kinds of backgrounds.

Maybe it was the mirroring. Maybe it was something deeper. But looking back, what once felt like survival has also become one of my greatest strengths. It allowed me to build bridges quickly—even when I didn't always fully relate, I could still connect. In some strange way, it made me distantly, wildly relatable. I could meet people where they were, because I'd spent a lifetime figuring out how to do just that.

But here's the thing: that same strength sometimes landed sideways. To neurotypical folks, it could come off as too much, too fast, or somehow not genuine. Like I was performing when I was actually just being me. That was the part that stung being misunderstood not for being fake, but for being exactly who I am.

One of those summer nights, we were planning to sneak out. The plan was to meet up at midnight, long after my parents had gone to sleep. But I was worried I might accidentally fall asleep waiting, so I set my alarm for 11:40 p.m., just to be safe.

Only... plans changed. Jennifer and I ended up talking on the phone and decided to head out early. So I climbed out my window into the warm night air, quietly thrilled by the freedom, completely forgetting to turn off the alarm.

While I was out roaming the neighborhood, feeling bold and untouchable, my obnoxious alarm started blaring inside my room. Loud enough to wake the whole house. Loud enough to make it very clear that I wasn't there to turn it off. My dad woke up and realized I was gone.

A little while later, as Jennifer and I were walking along a local road, a car pulled up fast beside us. It looked familiar. Too familiar. The window rolled down, and there he was.

My dad.

He leaned toward the open window and said, "Need a ride, folks?"

My heart skipped a beat, and my stomach dropped. We definitely didn't need a ride. We were having a great time, caught up in that sweet, rebellious sense of freedom. We were being "responsible," in our own teenage way: keeping to ourselves, staying out of trouble, sharing a few cigarettes.

But his question wasn't really a question. It was more of a command, he wasn't asking, he was telling, another motto from my childhood, so... we got in.

He dropped Jennifer off, and then we drove home in silence. I was terrified of how much trouble I was about to be in. But to my surprise, I was only grounded for maybe a week. Turns out, he was so scared I had actually run away that he was just relieved to have found me safe. And I felt bad for scaring him like that. It had felt like harmless teenage fun, but as a parent now, I can't imagine the anguish he must've felt in those moments, not knowing where I was.

My father was brilliant. Quiet, kind, introverted, witty and patient. He was the smartest person I knew. He got an almost perfect score on the SAT and swore the one he missed was an error on their end. I realized in my 46th year, about six months into my own autism journey that I probably inherited my nervous system from him.

His mom used to think it was funny to tell people about how when dad was little his food could not touch each other on the plate, it became a joke but it was serious business for him. When I think about it, signs were there. My theory is that because he lived as an only child alone on a farm until his sibling came along at age eight, his differences from other kids went undetected. His quiet curiosity flew under the radar and the farm was probably an ideal environment for him. I wish I knew, I wish I could ask him so many things now. I'm sure it was lonely at times, but knowing what I know now about neurodiversity, I realize it was probably a great space for his nervous system.

Growing up, the signs my dad was different were there, only none of us knew how to interpret them.

He loved his music and it was one of my favorite ways to spend time with him. We listened to song after song, sometimes just driving around with nowhere in particular to go, exploring back country roads. I learned about a variety of albums and musicians from him, from classic rock, to jazz, blues and current hits. We took turns playing songs for one another. He was pretty receptive to my music, although I think I mostly chose songs I thought he would appreciate, throwing in some Guns N' Roses and Prince for good measure. He was well-versed in music and he loved sharing that. I'm so grateful that he did, those are some of my fondest memories with him.

At the time, one of the most annoying things he did was to wake us up for church on Sunday mornings by playing Pink Floyd "Time" on the large Cerwin Vega speakers in our living room. It was an obnoxious and aggravating way to start a weekend morning, often our alarm clock to start getting ready for church. It was so loud and startling but ironically, it has become one of my treasured memories and I can't help but smile and get a little tear in my eye when I think about those days. When the clocks stopped screaming, I could take a moment to breathe and wake more peacefully, as I listened to the slower and softer instrumental opening of the iconic song.

It was usually a shitshow from there, with everyone scrambling to get ourselves ready for church. The scratchy dresses and uncomfortable shoes were just another additional layer of discomfort in the day for me. I wouldn't truly grasp my own sensory processing challenges until I started a long and lonely journey trying to support my children as they navigated theirs. As I realized some of their aversions applied to me too, I started to learn the terminology for my experiences.

I think my dad had these sensory challenges, too. I remember once he slipped a pair of Bose noise-cancelling headphones over my ears, excited to show me how it silenced the rest of the world. At the time, I didn't quite appreciate that hush the way I do now, the gift of an overwhelming quiet peace that instantly brought calm. Although, I did think it was pretty cool, it would be years before I had and could truly appreciate my own pair.

When we were kids, my parents smoked Salem Ultra Light 100s and by middle school I was stealing packs from their cartons to share with friends. They were disgusting and menthols weren't my first choice but, hey, "smoke 'em if you got 'em" right, that was the model. Anyway, in my bedroom was a door with a stairway to the attic. Ever since I saw "Nightmare on Elm Street" in the third grade, I was terrified that Freddy Krueger was going to come down those stairs in the middle of the night with his knife fingers and slice me up. I knew he wasn't real but in those grade school days after dark, he haunted me. I started tucking myself up so tightly in my comforter at night that I convinced myself no one could get to me. I would fall asleep so tight, with my little t-rex arms tucked up on my chest, that my upper body stayed in a tense state almost permanently.

So sometime in fifth grade, I decided to show that staircase who was boss and started smoking my cigarettes in there. It's sadly hilarious when I think about it now, but me and sometimes a friend, would go into that closed-off tiny space and crack the overhead door that kept the heat and cold out from the attic out so that the smoke could seep out and we would chain smoke cigarettes. *I probably need a lung scan*, even though I quit nearly 20 years ago.

It was in those same late elementary years that Sabrina and I started taking piano lessons. Mom would drop us off at Ms. R's house where she brutally conditioned us into keeping our wrists held high by poking them with a sharp pencil from underneath, on repeat, talk about an '80s nightmare. I loved piano, Ms. R., not so much.

If there is one thing I wish I had stuck with from childhood, it's piano. In sixth grade, I met Renee, who was an incredible piano player. She taught me hair band ballads and how to go to the store and purchase sheet music for current radio hits, a far cry from what I had learned at Ms R's house. As I leaned into my rebel side in sixth grade, I started banging out hair band ballads and other hits on the piano like "Home Sweet Home" from Mötley Crüe and "(I've Had) The Time of My Life" from "Dirty Dancing."

Renee and I did a lot of cool things, but one of my favorites was hanging out in the bookstore at the mall. We'd lose ourselves in the occult and new age sections, reading about zodiac signs, horoscopes, and psychic abilities, all the things that felt wonderfully taboo. Middle school allowed me to diversify my friendships more. I was rotating classes and meeting different types of people. Making a variety of friends allowed me to honor the varying parts of myself in ways I couldn't understand at the time. By then, I was getting bolder, engaging in riskier behavior, sneaking out and meeting up with boys.

The summer before my eighth grade year, a few months after my dad caught us sneaking out, Jennifer and I went to the Mötley Crüe concert. I wore a tight white skirt from 5-7-9 with a matching jacket and a black spaghetti-strap top. My bangs were teased high (full '80s edition) and I felt like a total badass. We knew we were in for a good night.

Jennifer's mom and stepdad had tickets to the concert too, but I barely remember being with them. They were drinking and partying too. Somehow her stepdad got into a fight and was tossed out of the concert. That left us middle schoolers, age 13, to figure out how to get home on our own.

I've thought about that night so many times over the years. How lucky we were. How grateful I am that nothing bad happened to us. It never even crossed my mind to call my parents. Probably because I knew if they found out Jennifer's parents got thrown out, I'd never be allowed to hang out with her again. So we did what a lot of kids did back then, we creatively problem-solved and figured something out.

Thankfully, we ran into a few older guys from our school. Now in high school, they were in eighth grade when we were in sixth, and one of them used to ride my bus. They tracked down some friends with a car, and helped us get home safely. They were nothing but kind and respectful. And looking back now, I am so thankful. That evening could have ended so much worse.

Situations like that concert are even more scary now for a multitude of reasons. As the mom of neurodivergent children, and a woman on my own late-diagnosed autism and ADHD journey, I had to unlearn everything I thought I knew about neurodivergence. For years, my understanding of autism was shaped by narrow portrayals like the "Rain Man" movie, which left a lasting, but incomplete impression on my generation. In reality, the spectrum isn't linear, it's circular with traits, strengths and challenges that can present in a wide variety of ways.

Much of what we've been taught about autism was based on studies of young, white boys, which means many girls and women have gone undiagnosed or misunderstood. We learned to mask, to cope, and to blend in—even when it cost us our well-being. I spent years in fear, as a young mom worried how I could protect my children from it. And it wasn't even what I thought it was. Instead, in my experience autism is a gift that we must each learn to work with in our own way. Like any strength, it has its challenges and extremes and uncomfortable parts. It must be cultivated and as a naturally curious researcher, I have been finding my way. It's been a journey of unlearning and relearning how to process the world in a way that suits me.

I have talked with multiple clinicians and my therapist, who say that diagnosis is just a label. And for a middle-aged autistic woman, there aren't great systems in place to diagnose, much less treat autism. In my experience, it isn't something you treat, it is simply part of one's neurological makeup. In my opinion, neurotypical people are often uncomfortable with neurodiverse individuals because they don't know how to receive or sometimes even respond to our differences.

The unmasked, unfiltered way that many autistic people express themselves—saying what we mean, showing up as we are, sometimes unable to mask—can be misread as awkward or intense, especially by those more accustomed to subtle social cues and indirect communication. I've seen this firsthand, both in myself and others. But beneath that rawness is a deep honesty and integrity—a kind of truth-telling that isn't rooted in social polish, but in a fundamental sense of fairness.

We've been told we are too much, too intense, too informative, too hard to take, especially as women. Our natural state is very contradictory to the messaging we've received for centuries that says, be easy, be nice, stay small, be quiet, don't make a fuss... well that just won't do.

To neurotypicals we can seem fake. To neurodivergent people, though, being anything other than who we are feels unnatural—that's what feels fake. So we mask and mirror. I've learned to mirror the mannerisms of those I'm with and with the safest people, I try on different mannerisms. I practice being other people, the ones I like best, so I can determine which feels most authentic for me.

It's hard to explain, because a common experience among what many people label as "high functioning" neurodivergent people is to be mistaken for "normal" or as someone without struggles or a need for accommodations. When you are in survival mode, you can't unmask. Unmasking and being yourself is a privilege, and not everyone experiences that equally.

GRAND THEFT AUTO
LUCKY TO BE ALIVE

I'm still 13. We're standing in a junkyard, staring at the remains of the 1986 Pontiac 6000 I hydroplaned a week ago.

"Do you know how fucking lucky you are to be alive?" my dad says to me. He doesn't speak to me like this often.

Can't he see I've punished myself enough over this? I've been torturing myself on repeat, asking—*What was I thinking?*

One of my quiet adolescent pastimes, something I'd only fully understand years later, was ruminating about social interactions, especially things I had said or not said or did or didn't do. Looping worst-case scenarios, rehearsing the consequences, replaying the moment again and again, like that scene with the car.

The insurance company's estimate of the totaled car's value is something like $116... an amount so small it makes me feel like I've destroyed everything: the car, my reputation, my parents' belief in me, my friends' trust, my future babysitting gigs.

I've quite possibly ruined my entire life. I'm convinced I've embarrassed not only myself, but my whole family.

I freeze. And I feel nothing but shame.

I haven't even finished eighth grade yet and I've already

wrecked a car. I could've been charged with grand theft auto. I only started my period a year ago and I could have killed my friend.

The weight of that, the weight of being so careless, so irresponsible, it sits like a brick on my chest.

And now I'm left standing here alone, absorbing the consequences of a decision I can't undo. I'm not sure why he brought me here.

Was it to make me feel worse about something I already know I can't take back?

The sky is gray.

It's spring, and there's just been a morning thunderstorm.

Yet, no one is talking about the part where six adults thought it was a great idea to leave two thirteen-year-olds home alone for a week, playing house with a two-year-old and a four-year-old while they vacationed.

Because 1980s parenting was a whole other level, that's why.

We raised ourselves, and we didn't talk about hard things.

They loved us and we knew that. We also kept up appearances.

Everything was supposed to look fine.

It was not.

So how did I get here?

First, I'll assure you—those babies are just fine.

A week before I found myself standing in the junkyard, we'd gone to my aunt and uncle's house to spend our eighth grade spring break babysitting for some extra cash. It was midweek, and after putting the kids down for their nap, boredom was setting in. We were out in the country, getting restless and were almost out of cigarettes. So we decided we'd drive a mile up the road to the "Country Pantry" store to buy more smokes, figuring we'd be back before the babies even woke up.

Wendy and I had become fast friends in middle school. We had several classes together and rode the same bus. Soon, we were having regular sleepovers, going to the mall and the movies, always finding ways to entertain ourselves. She was the perfect partner for a week of babysitting.

There wasn't a lot to do out there in the country in springtime. It was too cold to open the pool, and the week had been stormy, so we had to improvise. On this particular rainy day, a fine mist hung in the air, and the roads were damp. At this age, I wasn't yet aware of how slick wet roads could be or how to adjust my driving for safety in the rain.

I was taking the car out.

I'd practiced in the driveway and maybe a few parking lots by then, but this was likely my first time actually driving on the road. I honestly don't remember.

My friend adjusted the radio. We giggled, surprised at how badass we were in that moment.

As I hit the winding road and rounded the second curve, I accelerated just a little too much. The pedal got away from me. The tires slipped on the wet pavement. I overcorrected and hit the brakes—but it was too late. We were off the road and airborne before I could even react.

We were spinning.

Time slowed as the car lifted and rotated, the world outside disappearing. My life flashed before my eyes, as I sat in the center and the vehicle twisted around me. Like a load of laundry in the dryer—I was spinning and spinning, and I moved with the car, completely immobilized.

We flipped that Pontiac multiple times—six or seven, by my count. I was frozen as the car tumbled around me, each rotation letting out a new, violent crash of metal on pavement. Over and over. Again and again.

When the car finally slammed to a stop, we were upside down—in the back end of a parked car, in the driveway of a stranger's house.

I looked at my friend. She was out cold. Twisted backward in the front seat, her back against the dashboard, eyes closed—glasses still intact.

Oh my God. I've killed her.

She must be dead. It's all my fault.

I said her name over and over as I climbed across, trying to get out of the car. I hadn't been wearing my seatbelt. I tried to wake her, to get her out, free her, free us, from the mess we'd found ourselves in, in just a matter of seconds.

For a brief moment, I thought I might die. And worse—maybe I should have.

And then—her eyes opened.

Oh thank God. Someone must be looking out for us.

"Are you okay?" I asked, breathless. "Can you move? Are you hurt? Can you get out of this car?"

I wasn't sure if it would catch fire or explode. I'd seen so many movies, I was terrified the car might blow up.

With minor cuts and bruises, we climbed out through the window and pulled ourselves from the remains of what used to be a car.

Terrified, I walked toward the house whose driveway we'd just landed in, like Dorothy in "The Wizard of Oz." In shock.

I gulped, took a breath, tears streaming down my face, and rang the doorbell.

I don't remember who answered.

"Can I use your phone?" I asked. "I need to call my dad."

We'd landed on their property—just crashed into their random Tuesday like a natural disaster. A car full of kids falling from the sky. I'd hydroplaned us into the tail end of their parked car, in their drive-way, before lunch.

I felt sick. Still in shock.

I called my dad. He had a long drive to get to us—we were way out in the country. The ambulance and EMTs arrived first. Everyone was stunned. It didn't seem possible that we were okay.

But we were. A true miracle, they said.

The first responders told us again and again: we were lucky to be alive. The car looked like it should've crushed us. Instead, we walked away with a few scrapes and bruises.

Thank God we left those babies at home in their cribs.

Thank God we didn't take them with us.

They say I'm likely headed for "juvie" the juvenile detention center. Somehow, it's softly recommended that I ride to the hospital in the ambulance, that maybe it'll help keep me out of juvie. I think they felt sorry for me. I'm grateful for their kindness. The wreckage was so shocking, and I was clearly remorseful. I was so young.

I follow their advice. My parents arrive. I am heavy with shame and fear. I tell them the babies are napping. I don't remember much else —their questions, their reactions. That whole scene is a blur.

It was a miracle we survived. And all I could think was: *Where do we go from here?*

My parents were stunned. My dad always liked to remind us that we didn't come with an instruction manual and sometimes they didn't know what to do with us. I was certain this moment took the cake in lacking any sort of parental playbook. We were all out of our depth. They went to check on my cousins while I climbed into the ambulance and took the longest ride of my life.

That ambulance ride was one of the loneliest, most terrifying moments I've ever experienced. The isolation at the hospital was consuming. Minutes stretched into hours. At some point, I became afraid they weren't coming back. That I had embarrassed them so deeply, gone too far, and this was it... they might leave me here. Quit me altogether.

Where would I go? What would I do?

Maybe I was headed for that juvenile detention center after all.

It drove home a message I had received again and again growing up: *I am too much. Too sensitive. Too emotional. Too intense.* This time, I figured I'd finally pushed it too far that they didn't want me anymore because they didn't know what to do with me. I was too much trouble.

The clock ticked and tocked while I sat in the first significant, life-defining shame spiral of my life.

Everyone was stunned.

I was ashamed.

"If you had this same accident 99 more times, you'd be dead in every one of them. You and your friend are lucky to be alive."

Insert more shame. I felt sick.

How could I have been so stupid?

My inner critic had no shortage of commentary as I sat alone in silence.

Ironically, the very thing that was so reckless—driving without a seatbelt—may have saved my life.

What felt like an eternity later, my parents finally arrived.

My dad told me that what meant the most to him was that I called him first. That I trusted him in that moment. That simple gesture meant more to him than I could have possibly understood at the time. It didn't fully register for me until years later, when I became a parent myself.

At the time, he was deeply worried about the path I was on. And he believed that moment—the phone call, the accident, the ride, the whole terrifying spiral—changed my trajectory.

THE MAKING OF A MASK

My aunt and uncle, whom I babysat for, were always the kindest about this incident. They never mocked me, lectured me, or shamed me. In a week that could have cemented me as nothing but trouble, they chose compassion and that stuck with me.

From that first phone call—"Is everyone okay?"—to never bringing it up again unless someone else mentioned it, they gave me an unspoken courtesy I will never forget. Maybe they realized that a full week was too long to leave two 13-year-olds in charge of toddlers. Either way, I was beyond grateful for their response, from that first phone call when they asked, "Is everyone okay?" to never mentioning it again unless someone else brought it up. I always appreciated that unspoken courtesy.

My dad was right. That incident did change me—and my trajectory.

I'm pretty sure he thought it scared me straight. But looking back, it became my earliest and biggest shame story.

While he hoped it would keep me on the right track, it actually pushed me further into silence. I stopped making noise. Stopped making a fuss. I didn't want to be more of a problem than I already had been.

I felt like I'd already used up my lifetime quota of getting into trouble.

There was no more room for mistakes. No more patience left for me.

So I started shrinking. Hiding. Keeping things to myself.

Especially my emotions. Especially my burdens.

At least when it came to my parents.

They say kids who start drinking in adolescence are more likely to struggle with addiction later in life. That feels true in my case.

That car accident was a turning point in more ways than one.

Suddenly, I had an elevated social status at school. The wrong kind of attention found me. People started calling me "Grand Theft Auto." Some said "Juvie." It was new. It was shocking. But at 13, attention was attention, even though it was not the brand I wanted for myself.

And for a girl who'd been used to being overlooked, it felt like something.

I didn't understand yet that it was the wrong kind of attention. That it would steer me down an unhealthy path.

I'd already started dabbling with alcohol, thanks to early exposure via my babysitter, Mandy, again. I don't remember exactly when I first tasted it, but I remember that margarita at a friend's house. I remember sneaking bourbon from my parents' stash. They never seemed to notice.

Now, for those who don't know, in Kentucky bourbon isn't just a drink—it's part of the cultural landscape. Alongside the Derby, it's one of our state's calling cards. In Louisville, you can't escape it: the airport is lined with bourbon ads, distilleries are filled with tourists and top-rated hotels display bottles like artwork. There are bourbon tours, bourbon balls, bourbon pies—and always a reason to raise a glass. This would become etched into my subconscious as a pass for drinking bourbon, everybody did it.

I remember Mandy pulling my dads bourbon out and showing us the marked lines on the label, that's how you knew how much was left and if you were going to take some and didn't want them to notice, welp, just add a little water until you reached the line again.

And with that combination: alcohol, early trauma, and a brain wired differently than most kids, the perfect storm was forming.

One I wouldn't recognize fully until much later.

It was like an iceberg...massive, dangerous, and mostly hidden.

And I had gotten really good at keeping things hidden.

I masked what was happening inside me so well, even I couldn't always find it.

There was no amount of banging out hair band music on the piano that was going to keep me grounded enough for the path I was walking.

Not surprisingly, this took me down a path of lost identity and quiet brokenness.

I became a victim of my own bad behavior.

BAREFOOT IN THE HONEYSUCKLE

Luckily, we grew up on a 1.5-acre lot near the end of a winding road without sidewalks. We didn't live in a neighborhood, which I sometimes missed but I loved having extra land to explore.

Before that, my first home was a small trailer on my grandfather's farm. It sat tucked away halfway down a steep and rocky hill that took you to the fork where he liked to fish. The rest of the farm was surrounded by fields and even had a pond for fishing, complete with the slow rhythm of farm life. I was only two when we moved into the house I grew up in. Still, the farm would always be a sanctuary for me—my first home, one of my earliest ties to nature and a place I'd return to in life and in my mind whenever I needed grounding.

Since we were little we'd loved adventure in all kinds of ways—from catching crawdads in the creek to trimming out honey suckle bushes for a makeshift hideout where we'd lay in the shade, sample the blossoms, tell tales, read and do whatever else we felt like. Having that connection to nature was magic.

While I had dabbled with adventuring in the car, my sister, Sabrina had a much more intriguing mode of transportation. Sabrina had gotten a horse—something she wanted forever—and it became the coolest thing ever. Sabrina had loved horses for as long as I can remember. At first, she was able to keep her horse up the street, so she could go and care for her and ride her around the neighborhood like the baller she was. I wish I had more photos but some great ones live in my mind.

I simply can't explain how cool it was for my little sister to roam the neighborhood by horse the way most of us rode bikes.

Her friend Gillian lived nearby and they'd team up and ride across the empty fields between our houses. Out of nowhere, they'd appear—sometimes bareback—to tell us about their day. Looking back, I'm even more fascinated, because it was so damn cool.

We were free range. I didn't realize it then, but having that land and those freedoms was a game changer. It kept us grounded in the middle of everything else we were navigating. Sabrina taught me how to ride her horse, and I'd dabble in riding bareback too—but not like Sabrina. I idolized her: her bravery, her independence, her uniqueness, her ability to escape on horseback when things felt too hard. At least that's how it felt to me.

We were very different and I always admired that she got to do so many of the things I wouldn't—or felt like I couldn't. She was my first best friend, and I would have done anything for her. The responsibilities mounted. The older I got, the more responsibility I carried and the more freedom she seemed to have. Freedom she desperately needed because in reality she wasn't getting the attention and support that she needed.

By high school, I was grown by standards in our home. In fact, by the time I started high school I was drinking coffee and smoking cigarettes in my room as I got ready for school. I had friends who were driving, which meant my parents had to take me fewer places and I was living more like an adult attending high school— while Sabrina was still out there, riding across those fields, wind in her hair, the same way we'd once run barefoot through the honeysuckle.

One of my oldest friends lived just up the hill. Behind our house was a lot at the end of Cherry Ridge, where all the neighborhood kids would play for hours.

And most days, it seemed like the longer we stayed outside, the better it was for everyone.

That same eighth grade spring, not long after the car accident, the cable company had been working in the area, laying new lines. At the top of the hill, there were these massive wooden spools holding thick wire.

One day, a few of the neighborhood kids decided to stand one up and roll it down the hill.

It worked.

A little too well.

That heavy spool picked up speed fast and before we could stop it, it was barreling downhill, heading straight for our driveway.

I stood frozen, watching it gain momentum.

It was headed straight for my dad's white Mazda RX7.

I panicked.

I couldn't be responsible for wrecking two cars in the same season.

They'd give me up for sure.

In some ridiculous, superhuman burst of panic, I dove in front of it, trying to stop it.

It didn't work.

The spool rolled right over my foot, damaging my ankle.

That day, I cost us even more money with a trip to the doctor. They said it was likely a sprain, gave me an air cast and crutches, and sent me home.

Now I was a pain in the ass with a limp.

And it was twice as hard to get around.

CHI CHI'S, CIGARETTES,
AND THE BELVEDERE

I made it out of those crutches by late May, just in time to celebrate graduating eighth grade.

A handful of us girls rented a limo for the night. We went to dinner at Chi Chi's, played in the downtown fountains at the Belvedere, picked up a few boys, and took them for a brief joyride. Have I mentioned that I'm lucky to be alive? We were smoking, hanging out the sunroof, hooting and hollering as we passed people on the street. It was glorious.

That night, for the first time in a long time, I felt free.

No shame.

No panic.

No parents to stop me. They'd paid for the limo after all.

We closed out the night with a sleepover, and it felt like the perfect ending to the chaos of middle school. A proper sendoff—for a girl who had survived way more than anyone knew.

DISAPPEARING IN PLAIN SIGHT

I was supposed to stay in the advanced program and go to Seneca High School, but I wanted to go to Fern Creek, to be closer to home and with some of my other friends.

My parents didn't fight me on it. They let me switch.

Even though I was no longer in the advanced program and had been placed in honors classes instead, it didn't take long to gain a new identity. This was how I rolled into high school: The bad girl. The rebel. The smoker. In the smart-kid classes. At the time, it felt like a way to channel my inner badass—which is exactly what I did.

But that version of me didn't quite fit anywhere. Not in the classrooms. Not with the popular girls.

I became "the girl who smoked" in those classes.

The cheerleaders and dance team girls were friendly, but we knew I wasn't the kind of girl they wanted to hang out with.

And even though I was interested in cheerleading—I was short, preppy, and liked the idea of cheering others on—I didn't think I'd have the coordination.

I'd done it a year or two when I was younger, but the rhythm, the synchronized movement, the pressure of performing, the short skirts, the polished look that appeared effortless... it was all too much for me to keep up with. So I stuck to watching the games from the sidelines with friends. I loved the energy of the football games, everyone hanging out before and after.

Kids were drinking, smoking weed, hooking up, showing off. I never really got into weed. I hated the smell. The taste. The way it made my mouth dry. I'd need something immediately afterward just to get rid of it. It was worse than cigarettes and that's saying something, since I'd already gotten used to those thanks to Mindy's encouragement.

Weed made me paranoid.

Drinking, on the other hand, was a better fit.

It gave me a way to numb out. To quiet the pressure. To disappear in plain sight.

3

MY PERSONAL LEGEND
BE YOUR OWN BOSS & THE ADVOCATE

FROM THE TIME I was a young child, I knew I wanted to help people.

I've always been drawn to advocating for women, children, and anyone who's lost the ability (or the safety) to ask for help.

That instinct only sharpened after I was raped during my freshman year of high school.

I knew what it was. Even then.

But I didn't know how to say it out loud. I didn't know how to explain what had happened or how frozen I'd felt in that moment. And because I hadn't screamed or fought or run away, I worried that other people wouldn't believe me. Or worse, they'd ask why I didn't stop it.

The truth is, I didn't know how. I used my voice and my words, I'd said "no" multiple times, it didn't make it stop.

And that silence—the way I spiraled inside it—was its own kind of aftermath.

It shaped me. It taught me what isolation felt like. And it lit a fire in me to make sure others wouldn't have to navigate pain like that alone. My 1980s childhood had already prepared me to read between the lines, to hold things in, to mask what was really going on.

That experience only reinforced it. And this path, as messy as it was, was mine.

It was curated by the universe just for me. I didn't always understand it but now I can see how all of these moments carried me towards this version of myself.

A FIRE LIT EARLY

Later in my freshman year of high school, I gave a presentation advocating for *Roe v. Wade*. I loved advocating for principles that mattered. I liked explaining why rights were important and standing up for them in a room that didn't always agree.

Back then, I dreamed of becoming a psychiatrist. But eventually, I convinced myself I wasn't smart enough or wouldn't have the money to make it that far. So instead, I leaned more towards psychology, thinking maybe I could still help people in a more manageable way. This way would require less education while still making an impact.

I always felt different. Like an outsider looking in. But there were moments when I came alive.

Especially at concerts. I loved anything that gave me permission to express myself freely, especially live music, outdoor festivals, and big nights out. Music made me feel alive in a way almost nothing else did. Being in a crowd with thousands of people, all singing the same words, feeling the same beat, I felt connected to them in a way that was rare in the rest of my life.

Music cut through the awkwardness, the anxiety, the social rules

I never quite mastered. It let us feel something together, no small talk required. Concerts were like medicine. I didn't know it at the time, but they were a form of therapy. They gave me a safe, expansive place to sing loudly, dance freely, and release whatever I'd been carrying. No wonder I went to so many. They allowed me to unmask.

If only I'd realized then that I actually thrived in more intimate, often softer settings with less stimulation. I preferred one-on-one time with friends or small groups at someone's house, or in bookstores, libraries, parks, and creative spaces. Those were the moments that felt like home. I've always been someone who thrives in depth, reflection, and meaning but I often found myself with people who weren't seeking the same. I went to bars and parties because it felt like what I was supposed to do. Others seemed to enjoy it, and I enjoyed it too—but only after enough drinks to feel comfortable dancing and tolerate the assault on my senses. I did love dancing. It gave me a kind of freedom I didn't have in most other places. I was always self-conscious, though. I've never been great with coordination or staying on beat. But dancing let me feel free in a way that words didn't.

Still, on most of those bar and party nights, I secretly couldn't wait to get home. I'd slip back into my room, curl up in bed or the couch, and finally exhale. That was my true safe space. I suppose it was a kind of pre-digital FOMO. I thought I should want to be out there, doing what everyone else was doing. But most of the time, I just wanted to be home. And honestly? I've lost count of how many times I've thanked the universe that I grew up in a time that wasn't so easily recorded and replayed.

THE FIRST HUSTLE
AND A PARROT NAMED LARRY

My freshman year of high school was also when I got my first job outside of babysitting. I started cleaning offices for my grandfather on evenings and weekends with an older friend who could drive us there. It was pretty straightforward: vacuuming, dusting, scrubbing the bathrooms, and cleaning the floors. It was also the kind of opportunity I likely wouldn't have had if it weren't for my grandfather. There was only one downside: the desk of that one creepy guy who left nudie photos under his desk mat and in random drawers, almost like he wanted us to find them. Gross.

Still, I knew at 14 that this would be the first of many learning opportunities my grandfather, TW, would offer me. He was full of them.

"Be your own boss," he'd say, again and again.

He helped shape my entrepreneurial spirit by providing so many unique experiences, tiny doors that helped me build the foundation for where I am today. But more than the work, what I miss most about him is the time we spent together. The afternoons on his farm, sitting by the pool or the pond, or side by side on the couch while he watched Fox News and I rolled my eyes and challenged their commentary. Some of the best conversations of my life happened in those ordinary moments. There was laughter, banter, wisdom, and so much love.

Not long after he and my maternal grandmother divorced, TW remarried. Sonny has been my bonus grandmother for more than 40 years. She helped make the farm a home. Her impeccable taste brought a unique flare. In its prime, multiple peacocks roamed the farm and would call out and greet you on arrival. Those peacocks made a lot of loud sounds, they would call from the roof of the house to announce our arrival and even walk on the top of the car.

They were so majestic and beautiful to watch. We collected their feathers from around the farm and put them on display at home. We always wanted more of those beautiful feathers and TW told us if we sprinkled a little salt on their tails we could get one, such a trickster he was.

Sonny's heritage and cooking left lasting impressions on my childhood. I didn't realize it at the time, just how uniquely special and incredible a place the farm was to visit. Our holidays were filled with Korean favorites like Manduguk, dumpling soup, and Japchae, we would giggle and call it invisible spaghetti as kids. Then for dessert we would have Yakult, a yogurt drink or Korean popsicles. In the summer we would grill the best bulgogi you've ever tasted for cookouts and when we celebrated TW's August birthday around the pool, they were really special times.

Their farm was a sanctuary. I longed for it, especially after my mom died, the peace, the quiet, the Korean cooking, the comforts of a space that felt like home.

TW was a remarkable human. A hustler. A visionary. A generous, big-hearted man.

Being a grandfather gave him opportunities to do things differently than he had as a father. As a young father, he rose through the ranks to become the #1 salesman at a large local business, which allowed him to travel and build a better life, to eventually build his own business.

As a traveling salesman, he provided for his family, claiming the opportunities life didn't hand him. He had the kind of courage, confidence, humility and self-determination that made people take notice.

By 44, he had earned enough to buy a 100+ acre farm and build his own beautiful three-bedroom home: complete with an in ground pool, a brick patio, and a pond at the edge of Floyds Fork, where he loved to fish.

Fishing and hunting were two of his favorite pastimes. He eventually quit hunting and focused on fishing. I remember the way he'd prepare: a five-gallon bucket, a pole, some bait, a few snacks—he loved nuts and seeds—and off he'd go on his golf cart. Most of the time it was catch and release, but he loved the sport of it. He'd come back and tell us how many fish he caught, what size they were. He was a remarkable storyteller through and through.

He was so hilarious, often shrugging off concerns about his behavior or commentary with a casual, "Well who cares? This is who I am." He always had crumbs on his reading glasses, which hung around his neck when not in use. He once cleaned his cell phone with a toothbrush. Another time I watched him open a desk drawer, take a bite of a McDonald's burger, and put it back like it was nothing. When I asked how long it had been there, he shrugged. "Not sure," he said. I'm pretty sure he was teasing me, but you never really knew—he loved to do things like that.

One summer he left a fake snake in his preacher's mailbox. He was always pulling pranks with that rubber snake. One Christmas, he placed it on the shoulder of his life-size Santa in the foyer just to get a reaction. He was a true gem. One of the best gifts of my life really.

I smile with gratitude when I catch myself echoing his mannerisms—walking intentionally, confident and poised, with one hand in my pocket just like he did. Then I'll hear myself say something funny in his tone, like "Sheesh" or "Well golly bum," and it warms me from the inside out. Those little moments fill me with joy and bring back such vivid memories. I'm so grateful to have so many. One of the funniest was the time we took a work trip to China together that happened to fall over Thanksgiving. With the time difference throwing us off, he kept asking, "Is this yesterday or tomorrow?" He had this way of making the most ordinary questions feel hilarious. He brought a bright light to so many of my days.

He also had a whole fleet of vehicles for every need: a truck or a Blazer for hauling and muddy terrain, a car for everyday errands, and a golf cart for fishing or joyriding around the farm with the grand-kids. In the 1990s, he bought a late 1970s gold Rolls-Royce Phantom, and later an '80s model for Sonny. At the time, I didn't fully appreciate how extraordinary that was, especially because he was so down-to-earth and approachable.

He got a real kick out of quoting a 1980s Grey Poupon commercial, the one with two men riding in Rolls-Royces. With a big grin, he'd ask people, "Pardon me, would you have any Grey Poupon?" and then roar with laughter.

"*But, of course.*" he'd add, imitating the commercial's delivery, cracking himself up every time.

He even kept a jar of Grey Poupon in the glove box just for the chance to reenact it. He never sounded like that in everyday life—that polished, stuffy tone wasn't him at all. And that contrast was part of his charm. He was humble, funny, and entirely himself. That's what made him so unforgettable.

TW also had cows for years, another revenue stream that eventually became more of a headache than a help. They were always getting out of the fence, and the neighbors would call him at work to complain. He'd have to stop what he was doing and go wrangle them back in. The electric fence was supposed to keep them in, but it didn't always do the trick. By the late '90s, he'd discovered a hostess distribution center that tossed out day-old cakes, breads, and snacks. So, naturally, he started taking his small trailer to load up the surplus goodies and haul them back to the farm to feed the cows and fatten them up. At the time, I just shook my head and laughed. Another one of those wild, creative ideas from my grandfather. He was always full of surprises and kept us all on our toes.

He also had a parrot named Larry who lived at the office and kept everyone entertained. The best part? Larry could mimic TW's laugh perfectly. You'd hear him on a call, let out a loud laugh, and then Larry would echo it—and then TW would laugh again—and pretty soon the whole office was laughing along. He and my mom both had that kind of contagious laughter—the kind that could make you laugh before you even knew what the joke was.

SIMPSONVILLE SATURDAYS
NEGOTIATING LIKE A TEEN BOSS

By the time I was able to drive, my responsibilities evolved. TW wanted to start teaching me sales, so I began going to his office after school to learn the ropes and assist in the sales department. At the time, all the in-house sales reps were women; two of whom were my aunts, one married to my uncle and the other to my grandfather's brother. I got along with them well. Daisy was young and stunning and always lifted me up by telling me how beautiful I was and how much I looked like my mom. Dolly had a heart of gold and said some of the wildest, most memorable things I'd ever heard—she was truly one of a kind. Both were eager to teach me, and happy to pass along some of their accounts so I could start learning product lines and placing orders.

Now, I wouldn't say I had a deep passion for plastic plumbing pipe, fittings, or the loud noises and strong smells coming from the factory next door, but I knew the operation TW had built in less than twenty years was incredible. It was rapidly growing. Not long after I started in sales, TW told me he had another opportunity for me: he'd purchased a flea market booth to offload surplus and out-of-date inventory—including a growing collection of oriental rugs—and I was going to run it.

My job was to go to the booth on weekends, open it up, meet with customers, and sell the merchandise. I could price and barter however I liked, as long as I covered the booth fee and kept the business running. So, naturally, I decided to bring a friend along, pay her to help, and split the earnings so we could have fun doing it together.

On weekends, we'd roll the windows down, crank up the music, and head out to Simpsonville like the badass, independent teenage entrepreneurs we were. We'd open the booth like pros, talk with all kinds of people, and barter our way into extra earnings. It remains one of the most unique business experiences I've ever had—especially because I got it so young. I learned how to connect with people, sharpen my negotiation skills, cover my costs, and still have a few bucks left to buy the amazing fries at the concession stand. Honestly, I think a quarter of my earnings went to those fries—or another random flea market treasure. Worth it.

NEVER FORGET WHERE YOU CAME FROM

There have been so many moments in the last seven years when I've thought about my grandfather and all the opportunities he gave me that helped shape who I am today. What I treasure most about him isn't just the business lessons or big ideas, it's our connection. His time. His humor. His generosity with others. His wisdom. Like those of us old enough to understand, he was intentional, yet efficient, with his time. I used to call him like I would a girlfriend, only our conversations didn't last as long. I never understood why he always seemed ready to go—he'd say, "Thanks for calling," and wrap up— but now, in my 40s, I get it. It wasn't personal. He was glad I called. He just didn't have anything else to say, so unless I needed something, he'd talk to me later.

He always answered when I called. And he always opened with something hilarious, like, "Is this you? Why, you're looking wonderful!" I think almost every conversation I had with him started that way and ended with laughter. What a blessing he was. I miss his genuine heart, his visionary mind, and the humor that made everything feel lighter.

TW always tried to get me to come work for him, even after I started college to study psychology and justice administration. My grandmother finally told him to back off, to let me live my own life and make my own choices. My mom went to work for him straight out of high school. She got a Corvette instead of a college education. And I knew I wanted something different. I wanted to help people. I had been interested in psychiatry since I was fairly young, but the story I told myself was that I wasn't smart enough.

SMART ENOUGH ALL ALONG

We were working-class. We didn't have doctor friends or mentors who could walk me through the steps for medical school or the MCAT. And even if I had figured out the path, how would I have paid for it? I've said my grandfather was a successful businessman, and he was, but I would have never expected or asked him to pay for college. Instead, he gave us opportunities to learn when he could have just bought us more things. I didn't see a clear road to medicine. No one in my family had graduated from college yet. And at the time, it seemed obvious that the "smart ones" were my dad and my sister.

My dad was brilliant. He aced the SATs, missing only one question—one he always swore the test got wrong. He was quiet, kind, and genuine. A man of principle. And patient—my god, was he patient with us, especially when teaching us something new, not so much when we were testing the limits.

He taught me that violence was never the answer—but also that, as a woman, I should know how to protect myself. He reminded me I didn't have to take shit from anyone. He and my mom showed me how to stand up for myself. He taught me how to put air in my tires, never let the gas tank get too low, change my oil, think critically, and ask questions without fear. He taught me to appreciate all types of music and the value of a long drive on a beautiful day with no specific destination or timeframe.

GENERATIONS OF WOMEN

My mom taught me to be independent. She wanted to ensure I knew how to take care of myself and my children on my own. She drilled this into me from an early age so I'd never feel trapped—so I'd always know I had options. As a longtime credit manager at the family business, she taught me the importance of credit and having a personal cash reserve that no one else knew about. Always have money that's only yours, she'd say, for a rainy day or a swift exit strategy. Even if you never need it, always have it and have it easily accessible. She taught me Murphy's Law—that when shit could go wrong, it often would—and sometimes all you could do was laugh and hang on. Those were often some of the most character building moments.

She and my grandmother taught me resilience, and that strong support can make or break a person. With the right people around you, faith and a good sense of humor, anything is possible. If only I'd absorbed more of that earlier in life—instead of taking things so damn seriously all the time.

I have such fond memories of watching Golden Girls, Designing Women, and Hallmark specials with my mom. That's what it felt like being with her, my nanny, and my great-grandmother—like living inside one of those shows. Generations of bold, brave women laughing, crying, and sharing the complexities of life. Add in my sister and my Aunt Les, and it became something sacred. There was something holy about all those women in the same living room, kitchen, or backyard on Sundays, holidays, and birthdays. It's one of the things I miss most for my kids, those decades of strength, softness, humor and candor layered all in one space.

BOOKS, PLAY, AND THE TASTE OF THE HOSE

Both of my parents were readers. Some of my fondest childhood memories are Sunday trips to the bookstore, browsing the shelves at Hawley-Cooke Booksellers, picking out a few books, then heading home to read for the afternoon. I loved the comfort of it. The escape. Reading and writing grounded me. So did listening to songs on repeat and copying down the lyrics that spoke to my young soul.

Life in our house could be tumultuous. My parents were good people. They loved us unconditionally—which I've learned is more than many people ever get. I truly believe they did the best they could with what they had. But some days, the drinking and the fighting were too much to bear.

The '80s and '90s were something else. Parenting was much different back then. My first paid gig came at age five. My parents gave me a quarter to watch my newborn sister while they went two doors down to talk with a neighbor about babysitting us while they worked. It was fine, I spent lots of time with my sister already and loved being a big sister. I always enjoyed being around other neighborhood kids and my cousins. One of my cousins never even had a car seat—not just didn't use one, but never owned one. She rode everywhere either in someone's lap or just standing up in the back seat.

One of our chores included picking up cigarette butts from the yard. I'm still salty about this one, like they intentionally left them in the yard. Comfortable knowing they would just ask us kids to clean them up later. Additionally, I prepared dinner at least once a week, dusted, vacuumed, did dishes, and—of course— I often drank from the hose, I can still taste the metal. We played for hours in the concrete basement and did our best to stay out of our parents' way.

But there was a sweetness to that wild independence too. Hours spent roaming the fields that surrounded our house. Climbing trees —including the tall pine in our neighbor's yard. Building makeshift clubhouses under the honeysuckle bushes. Walking down to Miller Lane to play in the creek and catch crawdads. So much of the time, no one knew where we were. This was long before cell phones or GPS.

What a gift those days were.

4

FINDING FREEDOM
YOU GET ONE CHANCE

WHEN MY FIRST SISTER, Sabrina, was born, I was just five, and I treated her like one of my baby dolls. I played house with her, took pride in helping, and genuinely loved being in that role. By the time I became a big sister again at seventeen, it was a very different experience. Claire could have been mine and was often mistaken as such. This time around, everything felt bigger and more complex.

I learned my mom was pregnant during my junior year of high school. The room they were planning to turn into a guest bedroom was suddenly reimagined as a nursery. I was old enough to understand what a major life shift this was going to be, but still young enough that I didn't have the language or tools to process it. And having a mom who was pregnant and hormonal while I was a teenage girl also going through hormonal shifts made for some *intense* moments. We clashed often. The tension in the house was high, and our arguments took on a sharper edge. There were days when the air between us was thick with unspoken frustration, too much estrogen, and not enough room to breathe.

At the same time, there was a lot of excitement around the pregnancy. During my junior year, my parents started building a new house. My grandmother and her second husband owned a construction company, and they were building new homes at cost for each of their sons. For us, it meant something we'd never had before: more space. I was going to get my own bathroom and a finished basement where I could hang out with friends. It felt like a fresh start, a reset.

We moved into the new house in October of my senior year. In early December, my baby sister, Claire, was born. I was 17. During one of my mom's ultrasounds, doctors discovered something on her ovary—a mass the size of a grapefruit. The plan was to monitor it and remove it as soon as the baby was delivered. But when they checked again after the birth, they discovered it had already burst. Oddly enough, this was good news—it suggested it had likely been benign. Still, they scheduled follow-up appointments to monitor things. It was one of those details that reminded me how fragile everything can be, even during seasons of joy.

I loved having a baby around and my parents loved the help. They now had a newborn in diapers, a kid in middle school, and a high school senior. The following fall, I started college at the local state university. The most affordable option was to live at home and commute downtown for classes. I liked college—the big classrooms, the expanded curriculum, the diversity of people and their interests, and the freedom. I was drawn to psychology, especially human behavior and the question of why people do what they do. I learned 25 years later that psychology is a natural path for many neurodivergent people—often because we've been studying others since childhood, trying to make sense of social behavior and how to belong.

A sorority was never really on the table. It wasn't in our budget, and I wasn't sure how—or when—I could've fit in anyway. I was already working and just kind of wrote it off. Most people joined sororities when they went away to college. I stayed home, so I didn't even allow myself to consider it. My boyfriend at the time had joined a fraternity, but I didn't see much value in it beyond hazing and new ways to drink. Still, deep down, I would've loved to experience college with fewer responsibilities and join a sorority. But that was never really in the cards for me. So, like I had with the Catholic school kids on Cherry Ridge, I compartmentalized and told myself I was better off this way.

Instead, my college years became the next tier of adulting, full of responsibilities well beyond my years. When rush week arrived and sororities opened their doors, I didn't even think about attending. I didn't want to get my hopes up for something I knew I couldn't afford or where I didn't feel I'd belong. It became another thing that felt out of reach—so I talked myself out of wanting it. In my mind, the script became: I'm local, I already know people, I'll make friends. If I had gone away to school, maybe I would've participated. But I didn't. I stayed in the same city I'd always known. I don't even remember applying anywhere else. Leaving town never felt like a viable or affordable option.

I was on track to become the first college graduate in my family. I didn't have mentorship or connections to help me dream bigger. And so, like I'd done before, I quietly lowered the bar and kept moving forward.

What was incredible for me, though, was that my parents paid for my undergraduate tuition as I went, and I continued living at home until I graduated and got my first apartment. This allowed me to finish college without the student loans that many of my friends would be paying on for nearly two decades. I was grateful and intentional. Nearly every semester, I strategically signed up for at least 18 credit hours so I could drop a class, if I needed to, and still stay at 15. I built my schedule to span no more than three days a week. That gave me a few long class days, along with flexibility to work and be available to help my family on the other days.

So in the fall of that freshman year, I found myself settling into campus life. I loved the green spaces, the quiet corners, and the big library. I focused on my classes, made good grades, and gradually learned my way around. I remember walking into the library for the first time and feeling awed by the scale of it—larger than any library

I'd ever seen. I couldn't wait to call my boyfriend and see if he wanted to come study with me.

The problem was, I never really knew what he was doing. Since joining the fraternity, he spent more and more time partying, drinking, and doing who knows what. It was probably better I didn't know. I later found out that aside from whatever was happening at the frat house, he had also cheated on me with a girl we went to high school with—someone several years younger than both of us and still in high school.

That was the first of several infidelities with that boyfriend and I probably should have walked away. But I had so much responsibility in my life already that I found comfort in the familiarity of the relationship—even when it was toxic.

MY REAL JOY as a college student came in the spring of my freshman year, when I was ready to buy my first car as an adult. I wanted a convertible. A 1993 Mazda Miata, to be exact. I found one a few years old with about 35,000 miles on it. It was perfect for me and my budget. My mom co-signed the loan, I made the monthly payments, and just like that, I had my cute little jellybean of a car. That white Miata with the black top became my biggest sense of freedom to date. I loved the wind in my hair.

I'd wanted a convertible for a long time. I was sold on the Miata because of an ad I'd seen that spoke directly to my spirit:

"Before the spouse, the house, the kids, you get one chance.
There's something you should do before life hits you in the knees
with 10 bags of groceries and the need for a garden hose.

You should know how it feels to have the sun on your head
and a growl at your back as you flick through five gears
with no more baggage than a friend.

This has been known since the beginning of cars
which is why roasters were invented.
The Mazda Miata, the roadster returned."

I WAS SOLD. I had to have one.

It was pure bliss the first time I dropped the top, turned up the radio, and hit the road. I was on top of the world. There was something so liberating about only being able to hear the wind and the music—no interruptions, no responsibilities, just movement. It ignited my soul. That little car became a space just for me, one I didn't have to share. Sometimes I enjoyed driving it with a friend. But often, I loved being in it alone even more.

I had no idea how much I'd come to need that car—its reprieve, its freedom, the magic it held—as the next chapter of my life began to unfold. That Miata became both sanctuary and outlet in the weeks and years ahead. It gave me the power to take off when I needed to escape, to sing my heart out, to feel the sun on my back and the wind in my hair while the weight of my life loosened, even if only for a moment.

College is supposed to be about finding yourself—finding your tribe, building your independence, and making memories with friends. But for me, those years didn't look like that. Especially the "finding my tribe" part. While others were easing into adulthood, I was already living in the deep end—taking on responsibilities far beyond my years. That car became my refuge. My release. My way of holding on to my youth and myself.

Years later, I realized that I never formed the lifelong friendships that so many people do in college. This was for mainly two reasons, I had way more responsibility than your average college student and I am neurodivergent. It took me years to recognize this pattern, it was hard for me to go from meeting people I might like, to becoming friends, to actually becoming close friends. Unless a third person was involved that helped make this happen.

SMALL TALK HAS ALWAYS BEEN hard for me. I have always struggled with conversations that feel superficial or feel like noise instead of connection. Unfortunately, small talk is a common way people get to know one another. Probably another reason building and maintaining friendships can be so challenging for me. I like to skip the shallow stuff and talk about what fuels you, what are you most passionate about, what do you want to do with this one life we get and in this world. I want to understand your gifts and talents, see what we may have in common, and discover what makes you laugh and light up along the way.

When I do like someone, I often have so many questions for them that it can be overwhelming. I get curious and excited but that's not for everyone. In fact, to many neurotypical people it can seem weird or fake. They might write me off as high-maintenance, needy, or weird. But those are actually my gifts and strengths. I am a loyal friend and a fair and honest person.

Unfortunately, these qualities once opened the door for others to take advantage of me. I would miss sarcasm or subtle jokes. And I tend to take things literally, so I've learned to ask for clarity. I would assume people meant what they said and said what they meant. That put me in unfavorable positions—socially, emotionally, even professionally—especially in spaces where indirect communication or hidden agendas were the norm. I've learned to pay closer attention over time. And while that used to feel like a flaw, I've come to see it as part of my strength, my integrity, part of what makes me trustworthy. Still, it's not without its cost.

INVISIBLE BATTLES

A few weeks after getting the Miata, my mom was diagnosed with ovarian cancer. We were all forever changed.

At the time, I was taking between 15 and 18 credit hours at school while working part-time waiting tables at a local restaurant. I was still living at home, but I began to notice we were seeing less and less of my dad. I didn't have too much time to dwell on it—my schedule was packed. My baby sister, Claire, was about 18 months old, and I was growing even more involved in her care. My mom began chemo and the long, brutal journey of trying to poison the cancer out of her body in hopes of restoring her health.

They call ovarian cancer the silent killer. It's known for vague symptoms that can be mistaken for dozens of other things, and at the time, there weren't many reliable ways to test for it. It's also one of the fastest-spreading cancers. They caught it during a routine ultrasound. My mom had been getting six-month checkups since giving birth to my sister—partly because that last large cyst had disappeared so unexpectedly. This time, the mass was the size of a grapefruit. It needed to be removed quickly. And then the chemo would begin.

My aunt Les started coming around more to help us out. She and my mom were cousins but had been close like sisters ever since they lived together as teenagers. Les hadn't had a good relationship with her own mom, so she moved in with my mom and grandparents— and they'd been bonded ever since.

Les had been weaving in and out of our lives for as long as I could remember. She had seasons with us. Sometimes we wouldn't see her for months, even years—depending on where she was living. She was one of a kind and I loved her deeply. A great storyteller with an infectious laugh that made you laugh, too, even if you didn't know why. Her heart was enormous, and her past was heartbreaking. She would have done anything for my mom—and she sacrificed a lot to prove it.

Between taking care of my youngest sister and keeping up with chemo appointments, my mom needed extra support. So Les stepped in. She helped take care of my baby sister while my dad was at work and I was at school. I got my mom to nearly every chemo appointment, and Les helped her recover and made sure meals were cooked. It was both a sad and special time. Those ordinary moments of multiple family members navigating something extraordinary left me feeling oddly grateful—for our time together, for the way we all showed up. It didn't fix the devastation, but it helped make it bearable.

My mom had a full hysterectomy at 38 after giving birth to my sister, and the transition wasn't easy—on her or on our family. Now she was going in several times per week to have her body poisoned just enough to avoid killing her, but hopefully enough to kill the cancer. It was excruciating to watch her grow so ill after each round —and then be charged hundreds of dollars for medication just to manage the nausea.

I had always been close to my baby sister and loved spending time with her. But now, all of a sudden, in college, I was toting her around like she was my child. She was sweet, curious, and funny— often hanging out with me and my friends. I'd take her to the grocery store, to get her haircut, or to the pool to help her learn to swim.

That's when I started noticing something shift. Strangers—adults—began making comments. People assumed I was a young, unwed mother. Called me a sinner. Shamed me in passing, in checkout lines, with looks and whispers like they knew anything about me or my life. I was stunned.

Here I was, working hard to make the Dean's list, holding down a job, supporting my mom through cancer treatment, and helping take care of my sister—and somehow *I* was the one people felt justified in shaming at the grocery store? That was the moment I realized: I was not just outraged on my own behalf, but for every woman out there struggling and trying her best while being judged by people who didn't know a thing about her.

Were they getting this same kind of shame from the world?

I was floored—and I couldn't unsee it. I started noticing how people treated mothers using EBT cards, how they made comments under their breath in grocery lines, as if the government was doing them a favor handing out just enough to barely survive. It made me sick.

I'd always had a strong sense of justice, but this was different. This was personal. For the first time, I wasn't seeing these issues from a podium or a textbook—I was *living* them. The disconnect between how hard women worked to hold their families lives together and how little grace they were given by the world around them was infuriating. And it wasn't just my story I began to see how easily women in circumstances like mine—juggling caregiving, low wages, lack of support and relentless judgement —could fall through the cracks.

This wasn't where my passion for helping women began, but it was a pivotal moment where it deepened. My lens shifted. My fire grew.

I witnessed it in my own family—how those ordinary moments

that split your life in two, while navigating cancer, chemo, college, a young sibling to care for—could have sent us down a much different path. Without extended family support, friends to lean on or someone like TW who could help financially stabilize the transition my mom was facing, it would have been so easy to lose our footing. Easy to imagine a version of this story where we ended up homeless, unable to work, unable to pay the bills—much less afford the expensive medications that cancer required—struggling just to take care of ourselves.

As the treatments went on, so did the side effects. My mom began losing her hair. When it became too much to bear, she asked me to shave her head. She was tired of watching it fall out in clumps, so she decided it was time to let it go and start wearing scarves and wigs.

But her spirit was shrinking too. She knew something wasn't right with my dad. She had suspected something was going on—and then she got a call. Someone had seen him at a local grocery store, getting into a car with another woman. He'd left his own car behind, so this was her chance to catch him in the act.

So once I helped her shave her head, my next task was a stakeout. I scooped up a friend, grabbed a pack of smokes, a book of CDs, and headed to that grocery store parking lot. We sat and waited for his return.

THE BACKSEAT BREAKING POINT

It was a long afternoon, and it stretched into the evening. I don't remember how many hours we sat in that car, but it felt like an eternity. Then, finally, after dark—they pulled in.

I got out of my car, walked over to his, opened the back door, and climbed in.

"Well," I said, "you've been gone a long time. You're going to trade the four most beautiful women you've ever known... for her?"

I was hurt. I was devastated that this could be our reality, especially during such a heartbreaking time.

He looked at me and said "You're out of line."

"Really?" I snapped. "Mom has cancer, you have a toddler, and I'm in college taking care of both of them while you're out here doing whatever it is you're doing. And I'm out of line?"

I got out of the car, went home, and told my mom. She was crushed and in some way, relieved to finally know the truth. That moment only complicated things further as they began to move toward divorce.

The truth is, my parents' relationship had been toxic for a long time—and they both played a role in that. His relationship with the other woman had started before my mom was diagnosed. Her illness didn't cause the unraveling; it just sped it up.

That betrayal would complicate my relationship with both of my parents—especially my dad—for years to come. Months later, I told him I understood that people fall in and out of love, but his timing was really poor.

So I braced myself for the next season and worked to stay strong for her and my sister. My mom was only 40. She had so much life left to live. I was 19.

BETWEEN HOPE AND HARM

Once my mother completed her treatments it was a slow return to stability, good health and a sense of normalcy. My parents were getting divorced and our lives were changing. It felt hard to trust during those days, it was like waiting for the other shoe to drop. All we could do was keep putting one foot in front of the other, keep showing up, keep taking care of her and one another.

Her strength slowly returned, her hair grew back, her color returned and her skin began to glow again as she slowly came back to life. It was beautiful to watch her regain vibrancy. We all delighted in celebration as I graduated college on Mother's Day in May, 2000. She, TW, and my dad were each so proud. It was a beautiful gift of a day. Each of us thriving, we celebrated all my hard work of a season that suddenly felt lighter. Between her remission, my graduating with degrees in Psychology and Justice Administration this moment sparked a new season of hope and possibility.

I knew it was time for me to get a place of my own. I'd grown close to my new boyfriend, Adam, things had been going really well. We were thinking about getting an apartment together so I carefully began looking for a place close to home. They were building some new apartments about three miles away, enough space for my freedom and still close enough to be there if my mom or my sister needed me. It was perfect.

So I packed up my belongings and wrote my mother a heartfelt letter, thanking her for all the strength and wisdom she had given me. It was time for me to spread my wings.

"Don't worry mother, it'll be alright,
don't worry sister, say your prayers and sleep tight.
It'll be fine, lover of mine, It'll be just fine."
—Jewel, "Life Uncommon"

About the same time, my mom had started dating again, so she probably welcomed the privacy too. It felt like the next right step for both of us, even though we'd grown really close through her cancer.

Moving into the apartment and making it my own was an independent move I desperately needed after a season with so much responsibility. We bought some living room furniture and a dining table and I had TW over for dinner. As much as we all loved Sonny's cooking, he appreciated traditional home cooked American meals as well. I made roast, potatoes, carrots and green beans. It would be the first of many meals I made for him, homemade food was a love language I graciously shared with him.

For a while, life felt steady, almost like the hard seasons are finally behind us. As the months rolled on, I returned to a sense of normalcy. But stability can be fragile and mine was about to unravel once again when things took a turn with Adam. While bartending, he was introduced to crystal meth. His behavior suddenly changed dramatically, he went without sleep, became increasingly aggressive, and I started to feel unsafe. He transformed from the kind, attentive, and trusting man I once knew.

No longer the same person I fell in love with, Adam's entire personality changed quickly with addiction. I knew I couldn't live this way. The joint lease we had signed on our apartment further complicated things. One night, a bouncer from the bar where I was bartending came home with me. I was in the process of trying to get Adam to leave and things were weird. My co-workers knew what was going on and wanted to make sure I could get into my apartment safely and that I would be alone.

That night, Adam got angry when I arrived with Joe, the bouncer from the bar, who was very nice and just wanted to help me out. He yelled at us and even angrily took my sweet little pug dog, Happy, and threw him against the wall of our apartment. When he threw Happy, *time stopped*. My boundary suddenly became stronger than my fear—that was the final straw. I was done. That night I learned first-hand what I would later see in the faces of so many women in my work. How quickly life can shift, how suddenly a *before* and *after* can take shape.

I realized this was going to require an Emergency Protective Order, an EPO. I went to file one the following Monday. Filing that EPO was more than paperwork—it was the first time I claimed my own safety as an adult woman and consciously chose a future where I could breathe again. This experience only made me stronger, strengthened my voice and sharpened my immense need to advocate for others.

Adam moved out, with TW's help I paid him for half of the furniture and changed the locks. In that moment, I had what so many women don't—resources. I had a college degree, had studied the law, and knew my rights. I understood how to file an emergency protective order. I had a bouncer who helped keep me physically safe that night and TW's financial support to essentially pay Adam off so I could regain long-term safety.

Many women facing domestic violence have none of these, much less all three. And when children are involved, their outcomes are vastly different. I didn't know it then, but that experience would become part of the perspective I carried into my shelter days—an urgent reminder of how thin the line can be between hope and harm.

BROKENNESS, HER FINAL JOURNEY

Through the grace of God—as she would say—my mother made it to her five-year remission. In those few years when she was stronger, social again, and finding her way back to herself after navigating divorce, she returned to church and began making new friends. She even found love again. And that spring, she married for a second time. They celebrated and danced while Etta James sang "At Last" and we all toasted to the happy couple.

I don't specifically remember how she met Jimmie, but we were all grateful for the joy he brought her. It was a true blessing. He arrived after an especially tumultuous season and brought with him hope, stability, and love. He was good to me and my sisters, and he adored my mother. After everything she had been through, she needed that. We all did and we couldn't have been happier for them.

Several months after their wedding, we threw her a party to celebrate her five-year remission. It was early summer. The day was perfect—the kind Van Morrison sang about in "Days Like This." The weather was gorgeous, and the yard was filled with friends, family, and vibrant energy. It felt like a celebration of life, a new chapter. A full circle moment where the light breaks through.

And then, just a few weeks later, we got the call.

She was diagnosed with stage four ovarian cancer within weeks of her five-year celebration. The cancer had returned. It was aggressive. Within days, she was back in surgery to have a port placed in her chest for chemo. Radiation would follow. It was going to be brutal—but those were the only options.

The cancer had spread and was now invading her body and lymph system. Her decline was fast. By the fall, I knew this would likely be our last year with her. I wanted to believe otherwise—but it just wasn't so. You could feel it. The doctors told me the odds weren't good. Maybe a year.

She wasn't ready to know that information—not yet. Not after just beginning to feel like she could finally return to life. So she asked the doctors to tell me instead. She needed me to carry it until she felt ready to know more, ready to ask. She just couldn't stomach the possibilities yet. And so I held it—quietly and heavily. I knew her days were numbered. I'm honestly not sure if she knew or not. I think she did and was just in denial. Either way, it was gut-wrenchingly heavy.

I spent so much time that season watching her watch my youngest sister—through Halloween, Thanksgiving, Christmas. Watching her watch was one of the most painful things I've ever experienced. You could see it in her: the sadness, the grief of what she would miss, the weight of knowing. It funneled into her eyes. It was all there.

And then one day, she asked me flat out, "Am I dying?"

Open heart, insert knife.

I don't even remember how I answered—but I know I handled it with grace, with softness, with the utmost care. By that point, she was so heavily medicated for the pain that I was oddly grateful for her slowed processing. It gave me space to match my own.

I barely remember that Thanksgiving. I tried hard to make it memorable.

By Christmas, I could hardly keep my tears in. Neither could Jimmie.

I felt so badly for him. They had finally found each other, gotten married, and now she was slowly being taken away—from him, from all of us. It was heartbreaking to witness.

It seemed obvious it would be her last holiday season.

Cancer had become the big elephant in the room no one wanted to name—but it stole from all of us, right up until the very end.

You could see it taking her. The disease, the meds—they aged her rapidly, weakened her, hollowed her. It was one of the darkest periods of my life: so heavy, so heartbreaking, so hopeless. I tried to bring her joy, to offer ease and peace in her final moments—but it was exhausting. You don't realize it while you're in it. You just keep going. Living moment to moment. Showing up. Holding on. Confiding in friends. Creating joy where you can.

I cried in the shower. I cried in the car, top down, singing at the top of my lungs. Some days it didn't feel real. It felt like I was living in someone else's life, watching it all unfold from outside myself. How could this be happening? How could this be our reality?

I couldn't fathom losing my mother—not this young. Not for her. Not for my sisters. Not for my grandparents. Not for me.

It was crushing.

The winter was brutal, and she spent most of her time in her favorite chair in the living room—a brown leather piece with claw feet, its surface still new, leather she would never have the years to wear in.

In those final weeks, she knew she was losing the battle. She couldn't take it anymore. She was defeated, a shell of herself, exhausted. Cancer had stolen nearly every piece of her formal existence. Her skin felt cool and delicate, her body lighter than I'd ever known it, so fragile in my arms.

When the woman who gave you life begins asking you to help her end her suffering, where do you draw the line?

When the suffering becomes so deep and the point of no return has been reached because cancer is in charge now, where is the line?

She began begging me to make it stop. The suffering. The pain. The extinction of any kind of dignified quality of life was gone. It would not be returning. It became too much to bear. So instead, we prayed for peace, to expedite the process.

Meanwhile, I picked up the phone, called her doctors and insisted we increase her pain meds, the goal now was to keep her as comfortable as possible, but in reality it was anything but.

The increased meds did ease things a bit, and by the time the cancer had its way with her, she could have passed for my grandmother— her body frail and delicate beyond its years, her voice softened to that of someone nearly twice her age.

She was only 46.

That's how old I was when I started writing this book.

And I feel like I'm just beginning to figure things out—just hitting my peak. I can't even imagine the heartbreak and fear she must have felt, especially as the mother of an 8-year-old. It was too much to bear.

That year, my favorite album was "Spirit" by Jewel. Her angelic voice somehow covered the full range of my emotions—from "Life Uncommon" to "Down So Long."

*"Wind blows cold when you reach the top/ It feels like someone's
face is stuck to the bottom of my shoe
We've been down so long/ Oh, it can't be longer still/ The end
must be drawin' near"*

As we welcomed her final year, I searched for my spirit as if it were something sinking underwater. I imagined myself outside my own body, trying to push it toward the surface. I held it overhead in desperation, willing it to breathe. I gave everything I had, envisioning a deep gasp pouring life back in.

But even that was a struggle.

Would it be enough to keep it afloat? Or would I sink again—only this time deeper, more exhausted? Each round took more energy. I felt the weight consuming more of me. But I would not succumb. I would not let this force pull me under.

Because my mother taught me how to be strong.

My soul grew tired as the days crept on. I worked. I tried to normalize life for my sister, even when it was anything but. I sat with my mom, soaking her in—even though parts of her spirit had already begun to leave. I showed up for Jimmie, too, to help carry the weight. No one should have to live their first year of marriage like this.

So we looked for glimmers. We stayed close.
And we kept showing up.
That's all we could do, really.
Keep putting one foot in front of the other.
"Nothing could ever be enough right now."
I've said it a hundred times, but I push and push, and one day—I will resurface.

"Scars are souvenirs you never lose, the past is never far," cry the Goo Goo Dolls.

But I will prevail. I will survive—because the only way out is through.
Because of my mother and all that she has taught me,
I will catch my breath.
I'll never be the same—
Yet I will resurface.

My mother made us girls promise to dance. She shared the song "I Hope You Dance" by Lee Ann Womack and said her hope for us was that we live it.

A promise to my mother that I intend to keep. Even in losing her, she will lead me to the light.

When you're ensnared in the depths of trauma, you persist by simply showing up, taking one step at a time—tackling each task, doing the next right thing. You place one foot in front of the other, offering support, leaning on your friends and family, grabbing hold of every chance to laugh and cry.

Some days, I moved through life one hour at a time—savoring each fleeting moment on the good days. On the harder days, I clung to music.

Countless times, it was a song, a kind gesture, or a word of encouragement that kept me going. That season of my life was marked by living from one sacred, heartbreaking moment to the next.

On her final weekend, she was in excruciating pain.

The steadily increasing doses of morphine and oxycodone were no longer enough. She needed more relief.

So, on Friday morning, January 10, 2003, we called an ambulance to take her to the hospital. At the time, I didn't realize it would be her last visit. After meeting with the doctor, I was told we had mere days left—likely between two and ten. I was in shock. Even though I knew this moment was coming, nothing prepares you for news like that. Not about your mother. Sinéad O'Connor sang it best in "Nothing Compares 2 U".

She is your first home. The first person who could make everything better, just by being near. Just by wrapping you in her arms.

Just a few days earlier, Hospice told us we had a couple of months. But her journey had been abruptly accelerated. The countdown had begun.

If you've ever walked the heartbreaking and excruciating journey of sitting beside someone in their final hours—when their body is shutting down and they are in pain—my heart is with yours.

The final 24 hours of my mother's life were the most unbearable breaths I've ever taken. And many of them I took alone. My heart skips a beat and my chest gets heavy at the mere memory of it.

My mother was strong. Still very young. And even though the cancer slowly—and then suddenly—stole the life from her, she remained radiant in ways that broke me.

Those final hours are imprinted on my soul, softening only through time, and small moments of grief and release. The unwinding of that trauma—the way it gripped my heart—has taken decades to loosen.

In their strange symmetry, death is a lot like childbirth. You forget how excruciating it is until it resurfaces again—sharp, breathless, undeniable.

When someone's body begins shutting down from cancer, the disease takes up all the space and nutrients the healthy organs need to function. As her body began its final collapse, my mother suffered not only pain and exhaustion, but also delirium, shortness of breath, difficulty swallowing, and eventually—the death rattle.

Jimmie and I took turns, working in shifts to care for her. We were equally weary, heartbroken, depleted. Fueled by coffee, adrenaline, anxiety, and the hum of a dysregulated nervous system, I had no idea what awaited us that day. I spent most of it lying beside my mother, doing anything I could to bring her even an ounce of comfort.

They say hearing is the last sense to go. I don't know if they tell you that because it's true, or because it's comforting to those of us left behind.

But I clung to faith in that moment. I needed it to be true.

So I spent the day telling my mother all the things I needed her to know: How amazing she was. How strong and brave she had been. That it was okay if she needed to go. I told her how much I loved her. How much I would miss her. And that I would be okay.

Inside, I couldn't imagine how that could be true. But I had to let her believe it. I needed her to rest.

Each of us had our time with her. My dad spent Saturday

morning by her side. I'm sure he had much to say. He left by lunchtime and then I spent the day alone with her.

That was a brutal Saturday. She was so restless. She kept saying,

"Help me... help me... help me." Over and over, like a broken record. I didn't know what she needed. She must have said it a hundred times. I've never felt so completely helpless in all my life.

She cried out for her mother.

She cried out for help.

And there was so little that could be done. So I did what I could. I wiped her eyes. I swabbed water into her mouth. I put lotion on her skin. Neosporin on her scrapes. Cortisone cream on her feet. I played with her hair. I held her hand. And I told her I loved her—over and over and over again—like an even more broken record.

I did everything I could think of to comfort her. And even though she'd been sedated and sleeping—if that's even what you call that state—I know she knew I was there. I know she did.

Her final thoughts were about the beach. She asked me to help her into a chair. I said okay. And I think the last thing she said was, "I want to go to church." She was very out of it after that, not fully awake again.

But I know she heard me that morning when I said, "I love you." Because she whispered back, "I love you too." Those were the last words she ever spoke to me.

On Saturday night, around 11:30 PM, our favorite nurse—Denise —began her shift and came in to check Mom's vitals. She tried six times to get a blood pressure reading. Nothing.

I told her Mom's breathing seemed more regular. Denise listened, checked again, and quietly said the words I'll never forget:

"It's down to hours."

All the signs were there. And the longest she had ever seen anyone stay in that stage was two days.

Hours.

Just a few days earlier, Hospice told us we had a couple of months.

Yesterday, the doctor told me two to ten days.

And now—it was down to hours.

On Friday, my mom had still been awake.

I stepped outside, frantic and started making phone calls. My best friend arrived within minutes—thank God. I called my dad. I told him it's down to hours—probably three or four. I didn't know what to do. I asked him if we should wake my youngest sister, Claire, in the middle of the night and bring her in, knowing it might traumatize her? Or wait and hope Mom makes it to morning?

How do you tell an eight-year-old that her mother is dying?

Would she want to say goodbye? Of course.

But would it be too much?

My dad thought it was best to wait. She was spending the night at a friend's house. I said okay. Praying we were making the right call. Later, he told me he spent that entire night wondering if I'd spend the rest of my life hating him for that decision.

By morning, I knew we'd made the right one.

Next, I called my grandfather—TW. I couldn't reach my other sister, Sabrina, so someone left a note on her door. My cousin drove to get Jimmie, who had been sleeping and didn't hear the phone ring.

One by one, people started to arrive—family, friends, loved ones. My grandfather. Several of Mom's closest friends. We gathered around her bed. We prayed aloud. We held hands. We sang "Amazing Grace." She was resting. We each took turns leaning in, whispering softly to her.

Most of them promised to take care of her girls.

I told her, again and again, how much I loved her. How much I would miss her.

And I told her it was okay to let go.

I placed a lily on her pillow, hoping she could still catch its fragrance. My heart was breaking.

As we all joined hands in prayer, my cell phone rang—it was my sister Sabrina. My best friend answered. She told her to drive safely, but to come quickly. When she arrived, she sat beside our mother. Soon after, she climbed into bed and lay next to her.

Not long after, my high school sweetheart arrived. We weren't together then, but he'd walked so much of this journey with me.

Despite everything between us—the history, the hurt—he was still the one I called. Ours was a love as toxic as it was magnetic, the kind that makes perfect sense in the heart and no sense to its witnesses. But in that moment, none of that mattered.

He came straight from work. I stepped outside to catch my breath, and just as I pressed the elevator button, the doors opened— and there he was.

Standing there like an angel, right when I needed him most. It summarized so much of our relationship, the best and worst of times, the highs and the lows.

We embraced, and it felt like one of those movie-scene hugs— the kind that says I'm here, I see you, and I'm not going anywhere.

Around 3:30 am, my grandpa left, and I asked the nurse if we could move Mom to the middle of the bed so my sister and I could lie beside her—one on each side. I knew Mom wouldn't mind. We gently shifted her body, and then my sister and I climbed in, each of us holding one of her hands. I hoped to fall asleep there beside her. And I did.

At precisely 5:25 am, I awoke suddenly.

Something in me knew.

An inexplicable intuition told me these were her final moments.

We gathered around her. We told her it was okay to let go, that her battle was over, that she was deeply loved.

And then, in those final, fragile moments—she took three slow breaths, each one sounding like it could be her last.

And at 5:30 am on January 12, 2003, she exhaled for the final time.

In that instant, my world shifted.

And I would never be the same.

It was nearly two decades before I let myself fully remember why the day *before* her death always hit me harder than the day she died.

But my body knew. My nervous system remembered. Every fiber of my being held the truth. Because in those final 24 hours, I lay with her—through probably the most helpless-feeling day of my life. As she lay in pain, crying out "help me" over and over again, pleading for her mother—who was, herself, in a hospital bed across town—there was nothing I could do but stay beside her.

So I did.

I held her.

I ran my fingers through her hair. I whispered I loved her. I told her we would be okay.

I told her she could let go.

That is why the day before undoes me. That is why I feel immobilized—sad, quiet, called to rest. That is why I move slowly, gently, doing whatever I can to take care of myself and reach for something that sparks even a flicker of joy.

Because my body remembers and my soul longs for her and her peace.

It remembers the weight of lying beside her, alone at 25.

So wise.

So helpless.

And so full of love.

There was nothing I could give her in those hours—Except my heart. My arms. And my undivided, undying attention.

And I gave it all.

With every fiber of my being, I poured my love into her.

Moment to moment.

Breath to breath.

Sigh.

I did everything I could.

And I gave everything I had. I know this much is true.

And when I forget how brave I've been, I return to this day— and

I remember. How I showed up for it all, feeling fully and achingly alone.

* * *

Postscript – A New Kind of Remembering

Somehow, each year on this day, I forget why I feel off. I get gruff. I feel grumpy. Uneasy. And I can't quite place the weight.

So this year, I pivoted. On the anniversary of the hardest day, I planned something that makes me feel most alive.

We're going to Banff.

Ever since I first saw a photo of the turquoise lakes—especially Grinnell Lake along the Grinnell Glacier trail—I knew I was destined to go. There's something about alpine lakes, about the evergreens surrounding them. I've never felt more alive than I do in the mountains, in the trees, near water that reflects the sky.

So I did what my spirit needed. I planned a new memory—an adventure.

Because this is how I'll show myself, my children, and my mother how intentionally I'm choosing to dance in this one beautiful life we get.

CODA – FULL CIRCLE

As I edited these final pages—reliving the slow, aching hours of my mother's last day—my daughter asked me to come lie beside her as she drifted to sleep. So I did.

I lay next to her, writing by the soft light of my screen, holding the weight of one of the darkest days of my life while being held, unknowingly, by the quiet comfort of her presence.

It hit me like a wave.

As I remembered the bed where I once lay with my dying mother —offering her my love, my hands, my breath—I was now lying in a bed with my daughter, offering the same: warmth, closeness, a calm presence—offering her my love, my hand on her back, my breath.

Only this time, it wasn't a goodbye.

It was a continuation. A soft echo of what it means to love someone all the way through.

She didn't know she was replenishing me.

But she was.

It was as if the universe knew that as I poured out the memory, she would pour something back in.

A new version of love.

A reminder that I survived.

A reminder that I'm still here.

And still loving as fiercely as ever.

She returned me to my breath, after the retelling had taken it away—just like it had all those years ago.

5

LOVE, LOSS, AND POCKET COFFEE
FINDING LIFE AGAIN

THE NEXT COUPLE of years felt like I was just going through the motions. Especially that first year after my mother died. I moved through the world like a zombie stuck in a loop. I went to work. I came home. I showered. I read. I lay in bed, I soaked in the bath, then sometimes moved to the couch and lay there too, reading. I know I spent time with friends, but I couldn't have been good company. I was so heartbroken and raw, wondering if I'd ever feel joy again, or more importantly, if I would ever let myself feel it without guilt.

How could I go on without my mom? I knew she'd want me to but I didn't know how.

NO ONE WILL EVER LOVE you quite like your mother. My middle sister found a poem, shared it with me, and it stuck. I taped it to the side of a kitchen cabinet and referred to it often, reading and rereading it on the days I missed her most. Our version had a few altered lines and I liked it better that way.

Your Mother is Always With You
by Deborah R. Culver

Your mother is always with you.
She's the whisper of the leaves as you walk down the street.
She's the smell of fresh laundry,
flowers you pick, the fragrance of life itself.
She's the cool hand on your brow when you're not feeling
well.
She's your breath in the air on a cold winter's day.
She is the sound of the rain that lulls you to sleep,
the colors of the rainbow.
She is Christmas morning.

Your mother lives inside your laughter,
she's crystallized in every tear drop
She's the place you came from, your first home.
She's the map you follow with every step you take.
She's your first love, your first friend,
even your first enemy.
But nothing on earth can separate you.

Not time.
Not space.
Not even death.

I WAS HOLLOW. Broken. Surviving. And still, the days passed. Another year around the sun. I kept putting one foot in front of the other, slowly working my way toward some version of a new normal —a way of being in a life that would never be the same.

Then, one fall evening in 2005, I found myself in a minivan with a bunch of gals I didn't usually hang out with. Honestly, I don't even remember how I ended up in that seat. It was a divorce party for a girl I'd gone to high school with. We weren't close, but we had mutual friends. Still, there I was—along for the ride to celebrate her freedom from marriage.

At one of our stops that night, we ended up at this little hole-in-the-wall bar. I wasn't expecting much—just another round, maybe a laugh or two—but then, across the room, a guy caught my eye. He was with a few friends, including a girl who looked like she might be his girlfriend. I nudged my friend and pointed him out. She burst out laughing.

"That's my new boyfriend...and his roommate!"

My eyes widened. "Wait, your boyfriend is the one I'm interested in?"

Thankfully, he wasn't. It was the roommate I'd noticed, the one with kind eyes and a quiet confidence. My friend leaned in and whispered that the guy I liked was in a relationship, but nobody in their circle was especially fond of his girlfriend. She hinted that relationship likely wouldn't last much longer.

So, I made it clear I was interested and left it at that.

The following weekend, my phone rang. It was her. "He's single," she said. "Wanna meet up?"

I had plans earlier that night but told her I could swing by afterward. When I arrived at yet another hole in the wall bar, I spotted him at the pool table—but he didn't rush over. In fact, I waited 45 minutes for him to introduce himself while he kept playing. I was seconds from leaving to meet up with my other girlfriends at another spot across town.

"He's just nervous," my friend said, trying to keep me from walking out the door. "Give it a few more minutes."

I did. And I'm glad I did.

When he finally came over, something clicked. Instantly. He was funny, magnetic, and easy to talk to. The chemistry between us was undeniable. We spent the night squeezing in conversations between karaoke songs. Then, in a move so bold and sweet it almost made me blush, he got up and sang "Amie" by Pure Prairie League and "Melissa" by The Allman Brothers—the songs my first and middle names came from.

And he was good.

His voice was deep, warm, and confident—like he wasn't afraid to let me see him. Swoon. That kind of courage within hours of meeting me? I knew right then he was special. And I also knew—I just knew—this was going somewhere. It surprised me, how certain I felt. I didn't question it. I didn't overthink. I just followed the moment and trusted my gut.

Several hours—and too many drinks—later, I tossed him the keys to my convertible Audi TT and asked if he could drive me home. He was such a gentleman. Respectful. Steady.

From that night on, we bloomed.

It became a story his best friend loved to tell, always punctuated with the line: "And the panties just sucked right off of her!"

It wasn't quite like that though. We took our time. But the way he told it? Pure comedic gold. We cracked up every single time.

Matt and I got to know each other quickly. Just a week or so later, he met my dad when he stopped by my house on Thanksgiving. I had hosted and cooked dinner for my family, and when Matt was passing through after a gathering of his own, I invited him to swing by and say hello. From that point on, we were pretty inseparable. Most nights, we spent together.

A few months later, I learned that Matt had epilepsy—that he sometimes experienced seizures. I was caught off guard. I had never known anyone with epilepsy, never witnessed a seizure, and didn't fully understand what it meant. His friends made light-hearted jokes about it. His family spoke casually of it, as if it were a thing that just happened once in a while.

What I didn't realize then—and wouldn't fully realize until years later—was that they had never actually seen him have a seizure. They knew of his epilepsy but had never lived through those moments when a grand mal (or tonic-clonic) seizure took hold of him.

This seizure affects the entire brain and body. It is characterized by a loss of consciousness, muscle stiffness (tonic phase), and rhythmic jerking (clonic phase). They only knew the idea of it, not the full scope reality of all that experiencing one actually entailed. It would be years before I realized how much that detail mattered—how much it shaped their understanding, or lack thereof.

I wasn't sure what to make of it all or what it might mean for our relationship—or for a future we might build together.

But what I was beginning to understand was this: for the first time in my life, I felt like I was in a stable relationship. There was no toxicity. No chaos. No games. Matt was more steady and grounded than anyone I'd ever dated, and with him, I felt safe enough to set boundaries and name what I wanted.

And what I wanted was pretty simple.

I was living on my own—I'd moved into my mom's house after she passed, and I was making good money bartending before transitioning into a job at my grandfather's company. I had taken over the mortgage on her house, which was about ten years into a fifteen-year loan. I was building equity. I had a nice car. My life was stable. I had managed to put myself back together, and my independence spoke for itself.

I made it clear from the beginning: I valued my freedom. I liked doing things on my own. I wasn't interested in reporting where I was, who I was with, or why. I wasn't interested in anything other than an adult relationship built on trust. By 27, I'd been through enough fires to know I didn't need anyone to take care of me.

Although I didn't *need* a partner, I had grown very fond of Matt. I loved him. I wanted to be with him and see where it could lead. I've always been loving and fiercely loyal. If you trust me, and give me space to fly—then the possibilities are endless. When I'm in, I'm all in—committed, devoted, and solid.

But I also need my space. My freedom. They're not optional for me. They're how I protect my sense of self. How I stay connected to who I am.

I also had to explain that I came with a plethora of life experiences—and a complex past. I had an 11-year-old sister and an 8-year-old half-brother, either of whom I thought could end up on my doorstep at any time, and I would be responsible for their care. This was especially true for my sister. If something happened to my dad, I would become her guardian. I was already splitting time with her since our mother had died—my dad and I essentially shared custody during those early months after we lost my mom.

My brother's situation was different. I had no idea how his path might unfold if something ever happened to his mom. But given the possibilities, I needed to be upfront. I was in an unusual position for a 27-year-old—juggling roles and responsibilities that none of my peers were navigating, yet.

Ironically, that duality allowed me to fully embody the two identities I knew best: victim and badass.

I felt like a badass for surviving and for creating a stable, independent life by 27. But I also felt like a victim—grieving the heart wrenching losses that had shaped that very stability. As much as I had accomplished, it all came on the heels of profound grief. That paradox has stayed with me. It's a balance I've been sifting through for decades.

From the outside, I looked steady. Strong. Grounded. But inside, I was still filling voids—numbing out with alcohol, playing small, going through the motions. I had survived, yes. But I hadn't yet healed. And truthfully, I was standing at the edge of a very different path. I was within arm's reach of slipping into something else entirely—another life entirely, another version of myself.

Then came Matt.

I've always said: the fates took my mom too soon—and then they gifted me Matt.

Being in a relationship with Matt felt simple, clear, grounded. He was my lifesaver—there to keep my head above water. He showed up when I needed him most, with strong arms and a steady heart. He breathed life back into me. Reminded me what love could feel like again.

He scooped me up and pulled me back in. He didn't try to fix me. He just loved me.

And that love steadied me in ways I didn't even know I needed.

I was already in love by that point, and nothing could have changed my mind. But I couldn't have seen what the future would hold. I was in it before I even knew what I was getting into—my feelings had taken over.

The first six months were pure bliss. After so many years of heartbreak, loss, and caretaking—first for my mother, then for my sister—I finally felt alive again. I could take care of myself for once. I could think about my needs in a way I hadn't allowed myself to in a very, very long time.

It felt like I was reclaiming something—my ability to dream again, to plan my own life. A feeling I hadn't had since the early days of college, before my mom's cancer diagnosis turned everything upside down. For years, I had lived in grief. I had grown comfortable in it. I knew how to survive there.

So when joy came rushing in, I was scared. Scared to feel something that good. Scared to be that close to someone again. My nervous system didn't know what to do with happiness like that. And so—I let fear creep in.

I didn't know how to move forward without my mom. Up until that point, I hadn't even really tried. I had given so much of myself—my time, my youth, my heart—to being there for my mom, to caring for my sister, to holding everything together.

How could I be with someone my mom would never meet?

How could I *not* be?

I felt caught between guilt and grace—between the life I had lost and the one beginning to bloom. I didn't feel deserving of it. And I didn't yet know what to do with all the new emotions that were rising to the surface.

I was scared of feeling something so good and being so close to someone. And then, I let fear take over. I couldn't grasp how to keep my life moving forward without her. Thus far, I hadn't allowed it, I simply wasn't ready. I gave so much of myself and my youth to be with her, care for her, support my sister, and be there for her.

HOW COULD I be with someone my mom would never meet?

HOW COULD I *NOT* BE?

I SOMEHOW FELT undeserving and didn't know what to do with all of this new emotion I was feeling.

THE BREAKUP HEARD 'ROUND
THE BAR

Then Matt texted me and asked if I wanted to go to a Willie Nelson concert. In a moment of panic and denial, I pushed him away—refusing to let myself be happy. And as if that weren't bad enough, I broke up with him over text.

I know. Brutal. The worst.

I felt awful, but I freaked out. I didn't know how to handle this new love—this new chapter of my life that felt like it was opening too fast. So I ran.

He was shocked, as you can imagine. And ironically, the date of that breakup was 06/06/06—a sure sign to him that it wasn't meant to be. He was hurt, and so was I, but I didn't stop. I couldn't. I was in flight mode.

That summer, I tried to distract myself. I threw myself into my new job, spent time going out, meeting new people, filling my days and nights with anything that didn't remind me of him. But nothing felt as good—or as natural—as spending time with Matt.

So I did what I always do when I'm in emotional freefall: I worked.

It's a pattern I know well by now—when something is unraveling inside me, I throw myself into building something outside of me. I work to create, to achieve, to keep moving forward, while quietly dismantling parts of my personal life that might have thrived if I'd let them. It's how I've always tried to prove I'm okay. I measure my worth in what I can produce, even when my heart is breaking.

By day, I stayed busy. I'd just moved into the cabinet division—a rapidly growing department—and was tasked with establishing policies and procedures for managing high-dollar container orders. We were handling five- and six-figure sales, and the pace was relentless. Business was booming. Responsibilities were piling up. And I stayed distracted.

But the truth is, I worked by day and often drank by night. I performed the version of myself that held it all together, only to come home to the version that didn't. I carried the silence of my own unraveling in the evenings, trying to outpace the ache with a glass of wine, then another. It was a lonely cycle, but it looked like success on the outside to those at a distance.

I know now that I wasn't alone in that. So many of us learn to balance the weight of our personal undoing with the illusion of professional over functioning. It's a dance we do, one foot in survival, the other in performance—hoping no one notices how fragile it all feels.

POCKET COFFEE AND ANCIENT STONES

That fall, I went to Italy for several weeks to visit a longtime friend who had moved there with her husband. It was the perfect getaway —a break from everything, and a chance to reflect. We mapped out day trips, I packed my bags, and flew to Rome, where she met me and we dove straight into the city—touring ruins, strolling cobbled streets, soaking in the sights. It felt wonderful to be carefree in a place so far from my everyday life.

I adored Italy. The people were beautiful, the architecture breathtaking, the history layered and alive. We ate our weight in pasta, bread, pastries, and gelato—and washed it all down with house wine, espresso, and plenty of limoncello. This is where I discovered pocket coffee—those glorious little candies filled with espresso and coated in bittersweet chocolate. "Wakes you up or keeps you awake all day," the packaging promised. And I loved them.

After soaking up Rome, we hopped a flight to Sicily and settled into her cozy place in Mineo, right in the heart of the island. We cruised the winding coastal roads, exploring cities like Palermo, Taormina and Catania overlooking the Mediterranean Sea, stopping to marvel at ancient wonders like the Temple of Athena. It was pure bliss. I've always been fascinated by Greek and Roman culture.

We wandered open-air markets, sampling everything we could find. She even convinced me to try an olive straight off the tree—then burst out laughing when I spat it out immediately. It was awful. Apparently, freshly picked olives are completely inedible. She got me good. I chased it down with a pocket coffee, of course.

We toured a winery on Mount Etna, one of the most active volcanoes in the world. The owners boasted that the volcanic ash in the soil gave their wines a distinct flavor—and I believed them. The wine was incredible. The food was divine. The whole experience lit me up from the inside out. And as I flew out of Sicily, I caught a glimpse of Mount Etna erupting from the airplane window—an unforgettable sight and the perfect finale to an unforgettable trip.

I felt alive again.

But as the plane lifted off, I couldn't stop thinking about Matt.

I started wondering if I had made a mistake—breaking up with him, pushing him away. I missed him. I missed his humor, the way he made me feel at ease. I missed the safety I felt when I was with him. Things I hadn't known in a long time—some, maybe ever.

More than anything, I found myself wanting to share experiences such as this incredible trip with him.

IS THIS YESTERDAY OR TODAY?

I returned from Italy in late October, only to learn that we'd be heading to China for work. The business was booming, and we needed to tour several of the factories. Our Chinese colleagues had arranged the itinerary, and we'd be landing in Beijing just ahead of the Olympic Games.

From there, we traveled north to Harbin, near the Russian border, and then made our way south with stops in Jinzhou, Qingdao, Shanghai, and Shenzhen before finally taking the ferry over to Hong Kong. I was traveling with my grandfather and another man from our office, and we were joining a group of women from a partner agency in New Jersey. They took us under their wing and had organized a fantastic trip—balancing business with a few unforgettable sightseeing moments.

It was fascinating.

In Shanghai, we toured the city in a BMW 725i—stretching out in more legroom than we'd had in thousands of miles. We marveled at the scale and speed of development, the contrast between ancient traditions and ultramodern skylines. We were there over Thanksgiving and made calls home to family. That's when my grandfather started asking, "Is this yesterday or today?" It became one of his classic bits—a running joke he performed with perfect comedic timing that had us laughing for the rest of the trip.

China was extraordinary, and also sobering in ways I hadn't expected. So much was censored—we couldn't search Google, and the news was filtered. The rules were different. The access was limited. Still, I soaked up every moment. I was 29, halfway around the world, wide-eyed and grateful.

THE DIAMOND RING EFFECT

Matt and I found our way back to each other on his birthday—the winter solstice. I'd been reaching out for a while, and he'd been hesitant. Understandably so. But, by his birthday, he was ready to reconnect.

And when we did—it was heavenly.

It was as if no time had passed.

We slipped right back into us.

We spent the winter wrapped up in each other, more in love than ever. We enjoyed the summer together then fall came, and with it, football season—and suddenly, something shifted. This time, it was Matt's turn to freak out.

I was established. I had my own home, a good job, a nice car. On paper, it all looked solid. And I was ready—ready to start a family, build a life. Things were getting serious for me. But Matt started to question whether he was truly ready to settle down. By fall, I could feel it—something was off.

Then he said the words: he wasn't sure.

He'd met someone younger.

Someone not thinking about babies and mortgages.

He said he needed to slow down. Live a little more.

And then, just like that—he packed his things and moved out.

This time I was devastated.

I had finally allowed myself to believe in a future—with him, with us—and it all disappeared in a moment. I felt gutted. I was so vulnerable, I'd finally realized what I wanted, only to see it ripped away from me at a moment's notice. I remember wondering if this was how he'd felt the year before when I sent that brutal, heart-breaking text.

The next few months were rough.

I tried to distract myself, but my heart was broken.

I felt sorry for myself. I felt everything. I drank too much wine.

And then, winter rolled around again.

And like clockwork, he reached out. His heart had done its own unraveling, just like mine had the year before. He missed me. He wasn't sure he was fully ready for the life I envisioned—but he knew he wanted to be with me. He was all in.

I was skeptical. I'd been hurt.

But it didn't take long to feel safe again—in the cocoon of his arms, in the rhythm we always found together.

By April, I was pregnant but didn't know it.

And on Derby Day, our local holiday in Louisville, celebrating the Kentucky Derby, which always falls on the first Saturday of May, Matt proposed.

We were on our way to a friend's party, and he caught me completely off guard. He was nervous. It was sweet. It was just us— right there in the living room. No big crowd. No spectacle. Just love. He got down on one knee and asked me to marry him.

And I said yes.

Later that day, we joined our friends and celebrated—just in time for the 134th running of the Kentucky Derby.

Not long after the proposal, I had a miscarriage.

I was devastated. At the time, I didn't realize how common they were—how many women had gone through the same heartbreak.

No one really talked about it. It felt isolating and overwhelming. But we navigated it together. And without trying, just a few weeks later, I found out I was pregnant again.

I told Matt maybe we should wait to get married until after the baby came. He didn't think that was the best idea. He said we'd never want to plan a wedding with a newborn—and he was right. I'm glad I listened.

CELESTIAL CEREMONY

That summer, we planned a wedding in just three and a half months. The week of the autumn equinox, on a perfect fall evening in late September, we were married. The wedding was outdoors in front of a fountain, on the garden grounds of a hundred-year-old estate— surrounded by friends and family. Matt kept calling it the best party of our lives—and I suppose it was.

We were, in many ways, a constellation of opposites ourselves. He was born on the winter solstice, and I just two days from the summer solstice. Together we represented the longest night and nearly the longest day of the year. Stillness and light. Depth and fire. Somehow, we met in the middle.

But it was hard to get married without my mother. I left an empty seat for her in the front row, a visual placeholder for the space no one else could ever fill.

A string quartet played "Canon in D" by Pachbell, complete with a harp, one of my favorite instruments. I wore a strapless gown— part goddess, part warrior. I was rising from the ashes in tulle, diamonds, and grace, carrying every version of myself: the girl who had survived more than once, who had picked her heart up off the floor, again and again. The woman who had wandered the world, now finding her way to a new kind of home. The mother in the making. The one on the edge of her own unfolding—not quite there, but no longer lost.

My grandfather walked me the first stretch, from the house to the garden path. There, we met my father, who took my arm and walked me the rest of the way down the aisle. I gave myself freely that day. I wasn't anyone's to be given—I wanted that much to be clear. I was wise beyond my years, and some days it felt like I'd already lived a lifetime. Still, I was grateful for their arms guiding me with love to the altar.

We said our vows and stepped into celebration. Thousands of tiny bubbles floated through the air as we made our way back down the aisle. I lit up inside. I was ready. Grateful. Wide open to this next chapter.

I was 31 and four and a half months pregnant.

We honeymooned in Cozumel, Mexico—a perfect retreat after such a whirlwind season. Our room had a pool that flowed into a lazy river. We napped. We ate delicious food. We laughed. We exhaled.

It was peaceful, relaxing, simple and just what we needed.

We returned home, hearts full. Soon after, we took a Caribbean cruise with friends. It was gorgeous. We connected. We lived, laughed, and loved—just like my mother routinely reminded us in her final years.

I took it all in.

I had traveled across oceans, wandered ancient ruins, toured amphitheaters overlooking age-old seas, toasted beneath volcanoes and skyscrapers, arrived in Hong Kong by ferry, then reflected while floating in a lazy river. I drank wine in Sicily, sampled fresh pastries and pastas, tried countless new foods in Asia, and discovered espresso in the form of pocket coffee.

After all my journeys, I returned to my own house, married, with new eyes. I sat quietly on my own deck under the trees, listening to the flow of the nearby waterfall as the seasons shifted around me.

I was beyond grateful for a season of adventure. I felt blessed to have done so much exploring before the next season. We spent the winter nesting, preparing for the arrival of our precious baby girl.

Looking back, that time was a constellation of opposites—grief and joy, endings and beginnings, loss and return. I had broken a heart, including my own, and somehow still found my way back to love. I had mourned what could've been, and opened myself to what we were creating.

I stood in a garden surrounded by my nearest and dearest, the people who helped shape me, an empty seat in the front row holding space for the woman who made me.

That's how I found life again, not in perfect plans, but in presence.

Not in certainty, but in surrender.

Not in constant light, but in learning how to breathe through the shadows too.

Through reflection. Through movement.

Through darkness—

and the slow return to the light,

carrying everything in between.

THE LIGHT THAT FOUND ME

Our daughter, who we had already named Olivia, took her sweet time.

Three days past my due date—exhausted, uncomfortable, and more than ready to meet her—I started leaking fluid. My doctor told me that if I hadn't progressed further within 24 hours, I'd need to come in—for the baby's safety.

So I walked. I ate a big meal. I hoped.

She stayed nestled inside.

And so, we made our way to the hospital. My labor was going to be induced.

So much for my natural childbirth plan.

The Pitocin intensified the contractions and began to impact Olivia's heart rate, which was being monitored. I had a feeling it would disrupt everything the moment they hooked me up to it. As the medication dripped into my body, the pain escalated fast. Hours later, I received an epidural—my last shot at delivering vaginally. But the birth plan I had so carefully envisioned was being dismantled, hour by hour. It's funny—but not funny. And it certainly wasn't funny at the time.

But even in those early hours of motherhood, I was being shown something important: Our best-laid plans often don't stand a chance when life has something else in mind. Motherhood is both the most beautiful and the most important thing I will ever do, and by far the hardest. Never in my life have I cared more deeply, been tested more fully, or felt more heartbreak than in the sacred, tender, raw, extraordinary moments that motherhood brings.

It is everything: love and fear, pride and surrender, joy and ache —all at once.

Receiving an epidural was one of the most terrifying moments of my life, made worse when I learned I had to take it alone. I thought Matt would be able to sit with me, hold my hand, tell me it would all be okay. Nope. Not a chance. They made him wait in the hallway as I awkwardly leaned over the bed in a terribly uncomfortable position, a nurse I'd just met at my side, a tear in my eye, and a shudder in my heart. I felt small. Defeated.

I was so frustrated—so much of it came down to a malpractice liability. Things went wrong all the time. This was not part of my plan.

Minutes passed, and as the lower half of my body began to go numb, I realized I was losing control—of the birth I had envisioned, of the process unfolding in front of me. I called my sister, Sabrina. I called my best friend, Gina. She came and sat at my side, listened, held my hand while I cried, and helped me grieve the birth I had hoped for.

Around 24 hours into labor, it became clear I'd need a c-section. I still wasn't fully dilated. Then came the next blow: her heart rate dropped. Olivia was in distress. A c-section would be necessary for the health of the baby. I reminded myself: I did everything I could. I chose the right doctor. I chose the right hospital. I gave us the best chance for a natural birth.

But this is motherhood. The ebb and flow. The give and take. The joy and the sorrow. The gift and the challenge—and every complex place in between. Motherhood is a journey of learning, and our children become our greatest teachers.

They surprise us when we least expect it.

They make us smile when we need it most.

They bring us to our knees.

And they take our breath away—in both happiness and despair. They bring such a sense of wonder, they return us to our own forgotten magic. They fill us up and empty our cup, often in the same breath... with the simpler moments filled with beauty, awe, weight, and everything in between.

My final request—to hold on to some small sliver of control of my birth plan—was to listen to music as I was wheeled into the operating room.

The nurse shut me down immediately: "That's not allowed."

Thankfully, my doula stepped in. "We're going to ask the doctor anyway." The nurse pushed back, insisting it wasn't possible.

But again, my doula calmly repeated, "We're still going to ask."

And when we did, my doctor—empathetic, grounded, crunchy in the best way—smiled and said, "Of course. You can listen to your music."

I exhaled. A small victory. A much-needed comfort.

I reached for the hot pink iPod Nano Matt had given me. My thumb grazed the custom-engraved message: *To Amy Girl, Much Love, Matt*

I tell Matt I love him.

I tell him and our doula, that no matter what happens, through blood, sweat, and tears, I really want to breastfeed, whether I'm awake and remember the first time or not. They nod, understanding the weight of that request. They promise to do their best.

There wasn't much time. We needed to move quickly—her heart rate became irregular. She was in distress, coming out sunny-side up with a shoulder lodged. My doctor had to push her back in slightly to surgically welcome her through my abdomen. It took a toll—on both of us.

I braced myself.

    I wished my mother were there.

    I channeled whatever strength I could find.

    I put in my headphones and closed my eyes.

I smiled and took another deep breath. Then I hit play.

As they rolled me toward the operating room, I played "Keep Breathing" by Ingrid Michaelson—a song I've leaned on in some of life's hardest moments, when everything feels like it's spinning out of control. When all I can do is be present for what comes next, and... keep breathing.

I knew how the words would land as I welcomed this baby girl into the world:

"All we can do is keep breathing."

It was a song that had carried me through so much already—and would come to define so much of parenthood.

"All we can do is keep breathing."

The gurney stopped and locked into place.

    They moved me onto the operating table. The sheet went up. Suddenly everything was loud and clinical: metal clanking, fabric rustling, gloves snapping into place. So many new things, so quickly.

    I was fearful and exhausted.

    I had labored for over 24 hours, and all I want is to welcome my sweet baby girl into the world. But I already felt deflated. Defeated. Like a failure.

Heartbroken. Exhausted.

Then I looked up—and saw Matt.

My sweet, thoughtful, steady Matt.

He grabbed my hand, and even behind his surgical mask, I could see the smile in his eyes. He'd written "I love you!" on the outside of the mask. That simple act, that tiny gesture—it warmed me. It replenished my weary soul.

In that moment, I knew:

Everything was going to be okay.

As long as he was by my side.

And I was extremely grateful.

I smiled, and he squeezed my hand. I thanked him, told him how much I love and appreciate him. Thank God for our doula. He needed her just as much as I did. Because I'd already had the epidural, things moved more quickly. I played my song again, closed my eyes, and tried to escape the painfully bright lights.

"She's a she—and she's healthy," Matt said, holding her up and placing her on my chest.

I nodded. Smiled.

She was perfect.

It was still so bright. The faint hum of the overhead lights buzzed in my ears. I closed my eyes. When I opened them again, hours had passed.

She was nursing. My doula sat nearby, smiling.

"You're doing great," she whispered. "She's been eating like a champ. You did it!"

I looked down at her tiny face, her impossibly small body.

She was perfect.

And I slowly started to take it all in.

I felt *everything*—all at once. Tears in my eyes, disoriented from the medication.

Depleted from the trauma my body had just endured.
Grateful she was healthy.
Heartbroken that I missed the moment.
So full of joy.
So full of grief.

It was gratitude and sorrow.
Excitement and exhaustion.
All of it, tangled together.

I breathed. I looked down at her tiny head, her fingers, her body. She was lovely. And I was overjoyed. I was more thankful than ever for Matt. Never once did he try to make it about him—even though it was a lot for him, too. He never asked for a break. Never complained.

He listened to me growl and cry and ache my way through labor, through wave after wave of pain. And he handled it all—beautifully. Steady. Strong. Matt's quiet strength carried me. He was my rock. He cheered me on. Held the line. Kept showing up.

And in that extraordinarily raw, humbling, divine moment—
I knew: With him by my side, I could do anything.

A NEW SEASON

I moved joyfully through that spring and summer as a new mom, taking long walks and snapping tons of photos. I was embracing motherhood and finding my way into this new identity.

Matt was finishing his MBA—a great opportunity for our family, fully paid for by his employer. But due to a seizure he'd had when Olivia was six weeks old, he wasn't driving, which meant I was transporting him to and from class, with a newborn in the backseat, while trying to juggle everything else. Like so many young families, we were hustling to build something better for our kids.

A few weeks before Matt and I were about to celebrate our first year of marriage—just ahead of the autumn equinox—on an early Monday morning, I had just nursed Olivia and was preparing for work.

That's when I got the call.

My uncle told me that while my dad was on a fishing trip at his lake house over the weekend, he had died.

He was 56. I was 32.

And, like that, I felt orphaned.

This was a surprise. Like a punch straight from my gut and up through my heart. Although, by this point, my dad was in terrible health. His final causes of death were COPD, heart disease, congestive heart failure, renal failure and I think one other.

Five years earlier, in the year after my mother passed, my dad had an aortic dissection. It was another ordinary day, I received a call that he was in the ER and something was terribly wrong. I raced over to find him on a table, inverted. They had been running tests and recognized his distress. They were going to need to operate. Everything moved quickly and as they prepped him for emergency surgery. I gave the doctors details no one else had shared about his health that made an impact on the trauma to his body and recovery.

Because of his family's history of heart disease—and losing his own father in his 40s—he knew something was wrong the moment he sat down in his car to head to work.
Something was wrong.
So he trusted his instincts and called 911.
It's a good thing he did.

The doctors said timing was everything—and acting quickly saved his life. Only 5% of people survive an aortic dissection. He happened to be one of them. He lost the normal use of his kidneys throughout that process and spent the next five years on dialysis, which he had to have several times per week.

He was given five more years.
Five more years to walk me down the aisle.
Five more years to spend with his two youngest children—who were still just kids at the time, aged nine and six.

Now at his death, Claire was 14. My brother, only 11.

I think I just disassociated.

Somewhere beneath the layers of deceit, trauma, damage, and heartbreak, I knew this much to be true: His wife loved him—fiercely. Whatever else had happened, whatever pain existed in the past—she loved him deeply. And I believe she would have done anything to save him. Everything she could. As I grappled with attending yet another funeral of a parent—the final goodbye—I also mourned something more abstract, but just as real:

The loss of my first home.

The union that made me.

It was gone.

Completely.

Again, I moved through it hour by hour, day by day—just as I had with my mom. Only this time, I was parentless. And now, a parent myself.

The following month, we had our first long weekend planned as new parents—a trip to the Smoky Mountains with friends. We were looking forward to it, needing the grounding, the space to breathe before recalibrating for whatever was next.

Then on that Friday, just before we were supposed to leave, my younger sister called. She was distraught and scared. After an argument, her stepmom decided that there needed to be an immediate change in their living arrangements. Grief from losing my dad was setting in. I'd say we were all in the anger stage. That day, there was an emotional, chaotic scene that resulted in Claire needing a new place to live.

She was a bundle of emotions, angry, grieving, devastated. Heartbroken. They both were. It was just... too much.

Within a few months time, my stepmother lost her brother, her father, and now her husband. The latter two were sudden and unexpected. It clearly became too much to bear. We all have our breaking points . It was an ordinary day that became a before and after. For Claire. For me. Maybe even our stepmom.

There have been many times in my life when people tell me they can't believe the compassion I have for her after all the ways she altered our lives. But I lived enough to know that life is complicated, especially a life founded on complex trauma and children navigating adult experiences.

It's everyone's responsibility to heal their own lives, to stop playing the victim. You have to take your life into your own hands, find the tools you need, ask for the support you are looking for, and clean up our own messes. Like Maya Angelou said "When you know better, do better."

I have been an advocate long enough and walked briefly alongside so many traumatized humans in this world to know that some folks simply can't see past their own brokenness to heal. Or they have lost their ability to ask for help. I've seen this time and time again. That's when it becomes our responsibility as human beings to recognize our own privilege, to use our voice to empower others, and to speak for those who have lost their ability to advocate for themselves, who have lived lives we can't begin to imagine.

I have always said good support will make or break a person and that's absolutely true in my experience. So many people these days are ignorant to benefits and privileges they received that got them where they are. My sisters and I were lucky. We had family and we had each other.

In this pivotal moment, with Claire and my stepmom in crisis, all we could do was problem solve.

I called Sabrina, my middle sister.

Sabrina told us to go on the trip. "You need it," she said.

So we went.

And she moved Claire into our home while we were gone.

We needed those few days more than ever—to center ourselves before stepping into yet another season of caretaking and survival.

Claire was a freshman in high school. She had just lost her second parent. She told me to go. Sabrina stayed at our house, got her settled, and made sure Claire was as okay as she could be after everything that had happened.

We returned from the mountains and welcomed Claire into our home. Even though it had previously been her home, it was different now that Matt and I lived there and she was moving back in without either of her parents. So we did our best to make her feel at home.

We were now parenting a toddler and a fourteen-year-old—A teenager who had just lost her other parent, been kicked out of her home, and was barely a month into high school. We did everything we could to help her feel welcome. To create some sense of normalcy. To build a soft landing in the midst of so much upheaval.

We all moved through a bittersweet holiday season:
a first for us as parents,
a first for our baby girl,
a first for all us girls, now parentless.
Each of us carried our own grief in quiet, tangled ways—trying to make space for joy while learning how to live with absence and so much grief.

And then, a few months into the new year, Matt looked at me and said, "It's time."
I really trusted Matt.
So when, a few months after Olivia turned one, he mentioned he thought it might be a good time for a sibling, I listened.

"They'd be about two years apart," he said. "A good distance."
It felt close—maybe too close—but I trusted him. And I went along with it. We had no trouble getting pregnant again. Those who know me will think this was out of character for me, to blindly trust someone else with something so monumental, without much ques-

tion. But once again, I surrendered. I trusted. It felt like the next right thing.

On Olivia's second birthday, I started having contractions. That moment kicked off a long three-week stretch of Braxton Hicks and guessing games, trying to determine whether this time was *really* it. It was an exhausting few weeks of anticipation and discomfort.

One night, the contractions intensified enough that we headed to the hospital. But after an exam, they sent me home. I was frustrated. Tired. I hadn't been sleeping well. And as we left, I was suddenly overcome with an urgent need to use the restroom.

The nearest option? An all-you-can-eat Chinese buffet. The smells—already nauseating to my sensitive system—hit me like a brick wall. I made it to the bathroom just in time and proceeded to empty out my entire body in the most dramatic way possible. Vomiting. Diarrhea. A full purge.

My body knew it was preparing for something big.

Once things calmed down, I made my way back to the car. We headed home, where I spent the next 20 hours practically glued to the second hand of my watch timing contractions, waiting.

Finally, it was time.

They were ready to admit me.

Our baby boy was on his way, and I couldn't have been more relieved. I'd made it through another full-term pregnancy. I was uncomfortable and done and *so* ready to meet him. Labor took its time, but I got my VBAC—vaginal birth after cesarean—and that felt like a quiet victory all its own.

My sweet midwife stayed with me for more than six hours, helping prep my body and support me every step of the way. She was warm, attentive, and exactly who I needed. I wouldn't have wanted it any other way. In those final moments—early on a Sunday morning—I remember the ring of fire. And I laughed, right in the middle of it, thinking: *What the hell did Johnny Cash know about a ring of fire?*

A few more pushes—and there he was. My sweet baby boy. They placed him immediately on my chest and shoulder, still warm, still attached by the umbilical cord. He was so new. So perfect. They gently wiped him off as I stared in awe, present for every second. So different from Olivia's delivery—and just as miraculous in its own way.

Parker was my victory birth. The one that went closer to plan. The one where I got to feel everything to the end. Be present. Take it all in. I remember the rush of adrenaline. The wave of relief. The overwhelming joy of holding a healthy baby in my arms. I savored a glass of orange juice with pride. Stared down at this sweet baby boy. And let it all wash over me.

The mistake I made was thinking this pregnancy and delivery would be easier than the last. I told myself that because I didn't have surgery this time, my healing would be faster. Simpler. Less intense. But I overdid it. I didn't give my body the proper time to recover.

I pushed myself too far, too fast—a trap so many of us fall into as women. For me, the period was even more complicated by the timing. Right in the middle of it all, we were navigating the wind-down of my grandfather's business. The stress was mounting, and I found myself pulled in two directions:

One toward the sacred tenderness of new motherhood—

The other toward legacy, responsibility, and expectations that I didn't yet know how to name.

I still laugh thinking about the voicemail my grandfather left me the night Parker was born:

"Will you be at work tomorrow?" he teased, followed by one of his signature cackles.

He was joking, of course—and I knew he meant well. It was his way of telling me he loved me. He was glad everything went well.

TW was always good for a laugh. I sure do miss that laugh. Sometimes I can still hear it as if he is right there with me in the distance. But the truth was, these were high-pressure days. TW was struggling to keep up with the business, and he leaned more and more on me to help—to stand beside him in meetings with the bank, the staff, the consultants. He wanted me in the room for every big decision.

And in a way, it set the tone for that entire season of life.

I was doing everything I thought I was *supposed* to do.

I honestly don't even remember if I took a full six weeks of leave. It might have been closer to four—and even then, there were calls and meetings scattered in between. I do remember that Parker was six days old when I left the house with him for a meeting with the bank.

Six days.

It was... a lot.

I had the rare privilege of bringing each of my children to work with me during their first year. It was the greatest blessing and equally one of the hardest things I've ever done. I was deeply grateful for the opportunity, knowing full well that most women never get the chance. I witnessed so many firsts—rolling over, babbling, crawling.

I was there.

And as the months of 2011 rolled on, I became more deeply woven into the business acquisition and began working closely with new leadership. It was a season of transition, of stretching, of unfolding and discomfort. To show up. To keep placing one foot in front of the other. To care for my babies with just a bit of temporary nanny support.

To nurse them while juggling clients and consultants.

To keep myself nourished and hydrated because my body was constantly hungry from milk production. To stay composed and sharp while the ground kept shifting beneath me. You know what they say about early parenthood, "the days are long and the years are short."

I was reminded—again and again—just how remarkable women truly are. Our bodies are miraculous. What we're capable of, especially as new mothers, never ceased to amaze me. From making milk to functioning on scraps of sleep, we always found a way, even when it came at quiet, unspoken costs.

During my first pregnancy, we had modified my office to create space and privacy for nursing, napping, and playtime. Back then, my little pug, Happy, came to work with me every day. He had a bed beside my desk and made the rounds like a seasoned staff member—sneaking snacks, soaking up love, and accompanying coworkers on smoke breaks to stretch his legs and "handle his business."

When Olivia was born, she and Happy both came to the office. By summer, we had hung a swing from the tree in front of the building, where I could gently rock her when I needed a breather.

These were glimmers of joy in early motherhood—simple pleasures that anchored me in gratitude.

Then, in August of 2011, it was time to return to China—eight days away, over 8,000 miles round trip. I left my babies with Matt, their caretakers, and a deep freeze full of breastmilk. This time, instead of TW, I was traveling with the new ownership team, all men, of course. I landed late at night in an unfamiliar airport, accompanied by another American team member. We were met by a bus driver who didn't speak English. We didn't speak Chinese.

It was disorienting. Stressful. But I made it.

The next day, we joined another colleague. I was now one woman traveling with two men, navigating meetings filled with more men. Everyone was kind and supportive, and they made sure I had private spaces to pump. Still, I pumped 42 times on that trip to keep my milk supply steady.

Most women would've weaned by then—and I wouldn't have blamed them. But this is where my unshakeable determination kicks in. It's both a gift and a curse—that deep, unapologetic kind of grit that's equal parts love, fire, and follow-through.

As Matt likes to tell our kids:

"When your mother sets her mind to something, get out of her way and hold onto your hat."

I had committed to nursing Parker for at least a year. And I intended to honor that. So I kept going. I ate good food. I rested while they drank in the evenings. I grieved. I missed my family.

I felt for my grandfather. I couldn't imagine what it was like to spend half your life building a multimillion-dollar business, only to watch it dismantle as you neared 80. It was devastating.

So I played the part.

I did what I could to aid the transition, to support the acquisition, to carry his legacy forward, to help him keep his farm. He'd given so much to so many over the years. He'd done so much for me —it felt like the least I could do.

So, I traveled more than 8,000 miles and came home and nursed my baby like I never missed a beat. In some small way, it helped soften the mom guilt I carried for leaving them so young. I've never been more relieved to see my family than I was after that trip.

Those final months of bringing Parker to work with me—they were hard. They were the end of an era, in more ways than one and they're etched in my memory forever. There were so many life transitions during those few years. I had just become a mother—twice, three times if you count when Claire came to live with us. I was navigating the slow unraveling of my grandfather's business. I was showing up in boardrooms, pumping in bathrooms, and trying to hold it all together.

And somewhere in the swirl of it all, I became convinced that I needed a complete rebrand. That in order to be a good mom and everything the business needed, I had to shed the skin of my former self. I still truly believed that my past—my mistakes, my explorations, the voids I filled in my twenties, the things I tried as a teenager—disqualified me from being great at this.

Great at motherhood.

Great at leadership.

Great at anything with real weight and meaning.

Great at anything worth fighting for.

I believed I had to erase my history to earn the right to my future. And on top of that I had completely convinced myself that I wasn't qualified for these roles, but there I was, living them every single day.

As women we are told things like:

"You can have it all!"

"You can do anything that men can do."

"Be your own boss."

"If you can dream it, you can achieve it"

One of my most favorites, something my grandmother, Nanny, used to say with a smile:

"Everyone makes mistakes, that's why they put erasers on pencils."

She was filled with that kind of light. The soft, uplifting wisdom that wove itself into the tapestry of my life, quietly fueling me with hope and encouragement, even when I didn't know I needed it. My grandfather offered a different kind of support: practical, protective, proud. Together, they held me through the most tumultuous moments of my childhood and early adulthood. They knew how to lift my spirit when the world felt heavy, each filling my cup in a different way. And that's what I wanted for my babies. I wanted them to feel safe, lifted, loved. I wanted to give them sweet, steady memories—rooted in safety and softness.

I sometimes can't believe I convinced myself that, to be what they needed, I had to leave so much of *me* behind. The journey of reclaiming my power—of learning my worth and the value I bring to the world— has become one of the greatest gifts I can offer them.

I often say *parenting from a place you weren't given will bring you to your knees*. Breaking generational cycles is hard, slow, heavy work.

Yet somehow... I kept finding my way.

6

NOT ALL LOSSES LOOK THE SAME

THAT YEAR FELT like a slow surrender to the transition at work. I'd signed documents for my new position where the investors taking over my grandfather's business would retain my salary. The energy was shifting, and you could feel them taking over before it was actually time—but that was all part of it. Part of the long, drawn-out death of TW's company.

We were doing what had to be done so that TW could keep the farm, the place he'd been calling home for nearly half his life. I kept playing the part so he could keep the farm and his retirement. That was the deal we made: as long as we had a buyer, he'd be okay. He'd keep the land, his home. He'd keep the retirement accounts.

Not all losses came in the form of stocks and farmland. After decades of making his office a second home with collected pieces from around the world, TW brought a few of those treasures home before the business was gone. A handful of paintings. And one unforgettable eagle—hand-carved wood, nearly four and a half feet tall, perched on a branch with wings spread and talons ready. I don't remember where he got it. Sometime in the 90s it showed up in his office. It was definitely a statement piece. Now it lived in his dusty garage, because there wasn't anywhere to put it anymore. It looked best in his large office. Like a sentinel. Like it had belonged to something bigger, a grander stage of life.

Not all losses came in the form of wood or oil paint for me, either. Some arrived uninvited, in the middle of an ordinary day.

It was January. Early that year—just after the ninth anniversary of my mother's death—I got a call at work. ADT Security. Someone had broken into our home in broad daylight, just before lunch. The burglars shattered a full glass pane on our glass door in the walkout basement—the one overlooking the creek and the woods. Came right in. Walked straight upstairs to the primary bedroom, raided the jewelry drawers, and left in a flash. They didn't even touch the laptops, the iPad, or the flatscreen. They came only for what couldn't be replaced.

They missed only two things that day—two watches, both wedding gifts for me from TW's business partners: a dainty Omega Constellation and a bold white ceramic Chanel J12. Somehow, those remained. But the burglars took almost everything else I wasn't wearing that day.

Gone were the antique pearls my grandmother Iris had willed me. A platinum tennis bracelet TW had bought for her once, before it all fell apart. I'm not even sure how I ended up with that, I think my mom had it and it fell into my hands after she died. So much of my grandmother's jewelry had been taken by people she trusted, nurses and aides who saw her disability as an opportunity. She had good taste, a sweet spirit, and a slow decline. It made her an easy mark.

They took the tiny childhood earrings I'd been saving for Olivia —ice cream cones and cherry shapes from the 80s, cheap and sweet. Not valuable, just sacred.

Gone was the emerald that had fallen from the ring my Aunt Les gave me as a child, along with jewelry my parents had gifted me over the years. The diamond earrings my boyfriend gave me on my 21st birthday. My high school ring. A herringbone necklace. A rope chain with charms. A beautiful black pearl pendant that was centered in a diamond snowflake. A piece I picked out myself on our first trip to China in 2006. One of the few things I bought just for me.

They even took a simple green pendant I had picked up in Sicily for twenty euros—nothing fancy, but striking and one-of-a-kind. I adored that piece. Also gone. A beautiful diamond ring I'd bought for myself. Gold hoops. A custom-made amethyst pendant Matt gave me after Olivia was born—her birthstone.

Gone.

The police told me I should check Little John's Pawn Shop. My stomach twisted at the thought. But I went. Of course, nothing was there.

Eventually, we found out the thieves were a young couple addicted to heroin. They had children of their own. They started small—using their grandparents' church directory to find addresses of elderly parishioners who would be away on Sundays. Then the addiction deepened. Their break-ins got bolder. More frequent. So many that, by the time they were caught, they couldn't remember which houses they had hit. Mine was one of dozens, maybe more.

Can you imagine not remembering which homes you violated?

That's not a life I want for anyone.

Years later, I started receiving restitution checks. Small, but steady. They had gotten clean. They were rebuilding. Every time a check arrived, all I could think about were those young babies. I hoped it meant their parents were still sober. I hoped they were safe. I hoped they had a shot at a different story. They violated my home, and still, I found myself hoping they found one.

The worst part wasn't the stolen jewelry. It was the feeling that crept in afterward—like I had done something wrong. Of course I hadn't. But my soul didn't know the difference. I'd been victimized. It touched something old in me. Something wounded. Something I didn't even have language for yet. It lingered. It resurfaced on date nights, birthdays, and anniversaries, any time I reached for a piece of jewelry I no longer owned. Every missing item, a fresh reminder. Every empty box, a subtle trigger. A quiet little echo of shame.

I didn't buy anything to replace what I'd lost. I was a new mom. I didn't have the energy, or the desire. We had just enrolled Olivia in a Montessori school we loved—an unexpected expense, but one we were excited about. Our money went there. That's where our priorities were, focusing on what was best for our family.

On that cold January morning, standing in the wreckage of broken glass, looking at the mess they left behind and how shaken the kids and my sister were—I hit a new kind of rock bottom.

And for a moment, I let myself feel sorry for myself.

They left the watches but took everything else—and left me feeling like somehow I had done something wrong.

And in the quiet aftermath, in the unshakable stillness that followed, I started to feel something else, too. I began to grieve what I had been holding in for far too long.

Parker wasn't even a year old yet. Olivia was still two.

Claire was a junior in high school, trying to navigate life without her parents. I was too—only as an adult, it just landed differently. It didn't get the same attention, the same permission, the same novelty that grief does when you're still a minor.

I STILL FELT like an orphan too, a new mother myself, lacking her village, only people cared less because I was an adult. My grandfather, who had truly been like a second father to me, we were so close...had just lost his life's work.

And I had kept soldiering on.

That moment—the shock, the stillness, the feeling of being cracked open—it gave me a strange kind of permission to finally feel the heartbreak and the grief I hadn't had space to process. Not after work. Not after childcare drop-offs on the way to work. Not between chauffeuring high school social life commitments and extra curriculars, nursing, pumping, and making dinner.

I barely got to use the restroom alone, much less process the big hard things I had been experiencing.

There had been no room for it. But the burglary carved out its own.

And in that space, I finally let some of it go.

I didn't have language for it at the time, but I had been living in survival mode for years.

Always moving. Always bracing.

It was my normal—the only pace I knew.

The break-in didn't just shatter glass.

It cracked something open in me that I hadn't dared to touch—trauma. It would be years before I understood what it meant to feel safe in my own body. The year rolled on. I kept showing up, kept playing the part.

By that point, it was almost easier to follow directions than to lead. I was always leading things—at work, at home—and there was something oddly comforting about being given a task and just doing it. No vision casting. No decisions. Just execution. After everything the past few seasons had demanded of me—navigating grief, raising kids across such different ages, being everything to everyone—simplicity had its appeal.

That fall, my sister Claire started her senior year of high school, and we all took a Disney cruise to the Caribbean. It was a much-needed break. Matt and I stayed with the kids, taking turns mixing up the space between the two and we got my sister her own room. A couple of nights, she kept Olivia and Parker so we could rest. It felt like a gift—something soft in the middle of so much responsibility.

As Claire settled into her senior year, she was gaining more independence. It was a hard season for both of us. Tricky to navigate. We had done right by her. Matt was wonderful—practicing softball with her, tutoring her in math, encouraging her friendships, supporting her adventures. He'd even taught her to drive since he was much more collected than me. He stepped into the role of stepdad with grace and consistency. I had also tried to parent her as best I could, to be the support that she needed.

It was complicated. Going from fun-loving big sister to parental figure was a hard shift, for both of us. I remember telling her once that she had plenty of friends—but what she needed was someone who would help guide her. Someone who would teach her to write thank-you notes and remember people's birthdays. Someone to show up for the small celebrations and mark the little things with care. To be her own advocate and to bet on herself. To speak up and not take shit from others, those same lessons our parents had instilled in me.

Then there were all the things my mom had asked me to teach her.

That responsibility—carrying out the promises made to a dying mother—isn't something you can explain. It stays with you. I still can't fully imagine what it must've been like for my mom—to know you're going to die so young, with a daughter still so little. But I carried what she asked. And I did my best.

See, my mom had a whole laundry list of specific things she wanted me to take care of.

Make sure I looked after my sister.

Make sure my father handled things. And if there was ever a question—a gap—I was supposed to step in. To support my sister. To provide for her if needed.

My mom had a life insurance policy and we were each to receive a little money. But I was trusted to be thoughtful and careful. To invest her money on my sister's behalf, so she'd have something waiting for her. She asked me to take all her jewelry and place it in a lockbox. To keep it safe. I had received the diamond ring my father had given her and Sabrina had gotten the ring from my mom's first engagement, years before my dad. Because of this, my youngest sister was to get everything else of value from my mom. My job was to collect those pieces, secure them, and keep them a secret until my sister was old enough to manage them on her own, whatever age that was.

According to my mom's will, that age was 21.

Not an age I'd recommend entrusting money and valuables to a person, but I didn't make the rules, I just abided by them.

Our mom also made a list—antiques, collectibles, the higher-value items. I was supposed to know who got what. I was to divide the contents of the house fairly. Handle the logistics. Be the executor. That didn't even count the massive undertaking of being the one who took over the house. It was my job to go through all the items, furniture, clothes, and keepsakes my mom had amassed over her 46 years of life.

IN 2009, Matt and I bought my sisters out of the house, taking over the mortgage. There had been equity in it, so we each received a share. But I was the oldest. The one in charge. The one carrying out the requests with an attorney and the will.

There was so much pressure in that list. So many rules. So many expectations.

But I hadn't yet lived enough life, hadn't learned enough patience or grace to fully embody what that role required.

I was so heartbroken.

And I did the best I could with what I had.

That's all I could do.

In some ways, it took a toll on my relationship with my Claire.

But as the years ticked on—and she eventually became a mom herself—she started to understand.

That doesn't mean the early years were any easier.

By spring break of her senior year, my sister decided to move back in with her stepmom. At that point, she was 18, and there wasn't much to be done. Not long after Claire graduated, she was packing for college—heading to the University of Kentucky that fall. Wide open spaces. A fresh start. Her own chapter. We were all excited for her.

And somehow, we'd done it.

Aside from losing her parents, Claire graduated high school in a great space. She never got into much trouble, had found great friends, wasn't a drinker, didn't do drugs, and hadn't gotten pregnant—she had done things right.

And we had helped her reach adulthood without any additional trauma, aside from the occasional seizure Matt would experience.

It felt like a win in our book. And we were happy to watch her step into the next chapter.

Around the same time, we knew it was time to sell the house. We had loved that house—the one my parents designed together, hand-selecting the paint, wallpaper, fixtures, and appliances, while my mom was pregnant with Claire. They found out in time to turn the guest bedroom into a nursery. Even the lot was an intentional piece of land, with a stream and woods in the back and the beautiful sound of a rushing waterfall. It was gorgeous.

When I painted the primary bedroom in an effort to make it more my own, I added something small and sacred: a heart, hand-painted in a red-pink color, about four and a half feet from the ground, tucked just behind the French door on the right.

A quiet mark that love had lived here in many forms.

I wasn't painting over my mom—I was moving into the next season, one where I carried her in my heart.

But the truth was, we didn't do anything in that end of town anymore, and traffic had become a real headache. More importantly, we knew it was time to downsize. Parker would be starting the Montessori soon, and that meant a second tuition to add to the budget. The expenses were piling up.

So, I finished the last of the heavy sentimental work—sifting through what remained of my mother's things. What did I want to keep? What could I pass on? What deserved a last-call message to ask if anyone still wanted it?

I still look back and don't know how I did it—working full-time while packing up that 4,200-square-foot house filled with her 46 years of life and my 35. I really don't know how I managed it, but I did.

I must have taken ten loads to Goodwill, with another big bundle headed to Dress for Success. The trickiest part was the house we had our eye on was tied up in court and the purchase was going to take awhile. So, we packed up most of our belongings, put them in storage, and moved into my in-laws' basement. They graciously took us in while we waited for three months.

We had the basement to ourselves. It was basically a full apartment. We moved in the last week of October, just before Halloween. In early January, we closed on our house—but stayed with my in-laws another month while we remodeled. There was no way I was doing a kitchen renovation with a two and four-year-old who ate every other hour.

Parker joined Olivia at the Montessori school that January. We had dinner and worked on the new house in the evenings after school pick-up and spent nights in my in-laws basement. We'd complete a few hours of work, bathe the kids there, get them in pajamas, then head back to my in-laws' just in time to tuck them into bed.

We did a lot of the demo, the cleaning, and some of the renovation work ourselves. I still don't know how we managed to pack up an entire life, squeeze into a basement, and remodel a house while raising two toddlers, but we did.

We were building our future.

We moved into our new home in the first week of February, 2014, and there was snow on the ground for what felt like the entire month —much more than usual for your average Kentucky winter. That meant moving into a new home with new floors—and lots of wet snow to clean up. But we were excited and proud. And for the first time as a married couple, it allowed us to really create something of our own.

Matt and I lived in my mom's house for years, surrounded by her things. Her art, her dishes, her furniture—each piece held a memory, a story, a weight. It didn't feel right to replace her nice things with new ones just to make a space feel different. Because it wasn't just someone else's house—it was hers. And in so many ways, it became mine too. Living there was about honoring her. Honoring what she asked me to do for Claire. Honoring her memory, her space, their legacy. There was a lot of heavy, unspoken commitment in that house which I didn't fully grasp at the time because I was still buried in heartbreak and loss.

Moving out was hard. It felt like a final severing.

I had lost my mom. Then my dad. And now, I was giving up the last home I had ever known as a child—even though I was already 17 when we moved in. For someone with such a longing for nostalgia it was tough.

This made everything real. There would be no home to return to. No place that held the old versions of me or my sisters. It was closure in the truest sense. But now, for the first time, we were stepping into something that was ours. And that felt good. It was a fresh beginning. And it was ours.

That month, we also celebrated Olivia and Parker's birthdays as they turned three and five. My little pug was getting old. He enjoyed his later years, but by then he was fourteen. We lost him the following winter and buried him in the backyard of our new house. I still remember watching Parker make little trips in his rain boots and umbrella to the spot in the backyard, quietly saying his goodbyes and well wishes.

And just like that, I found myself settled into motherhood—and complacent in a job I'd grown to dislike.

Looking back, I wasn't truly stuck. We always have a choice. But I had just walked through something traumatic. I had watched my grandfather lose his life's work. Our relationship suffered in the process because I was both his safe space and the one person who saw, clearly and completely, what was happening with the company behind the scenes. I became his advocate. And I know that was hard on him. I can't even imagine the heartbreak he carried.

Part of the reason why I stayed with the new company was because I was tired. I was a young mother who had just watched a man I had put on a pedestal my whole life lose everything he'd built, right before my eyes. I hadn't reclaimed my power yet. I was grieving, drained, and doing my best to be a good mom and a good wife.

What I did know was how much I loved that Montessori school. I would've done anything to keep the kids there. They spent their mornings immersed in "practical life" work—grinding coffee beans, learning how to sew, doing math with extraordinary visual materials. They learned cursive by tracing letters with their fingers in sand. They drank from real glasses, and when someone spilled one, they fetched a mop and proudly cleaned it up.

There was such joy in the simplicity, in the way they were trusted with real community work. In the afternoons, they were outside— climbing trees, tending a garden, learning how to be in the world with both curiosity and care. It felt like what childhood was supposed to be. It was exactly what we wanted for them.

I'll never forget how the school moved us the first time we visited. We knew immediately—that was where we wanted our kids to go.

And as Feist sings, we collected the moments, one by one.

WHAT'S NEXT?

I spent so many years holding everything together.

I lost my mother. Then I lost her mother, my beloved Nanny. Then, I almost lost my father with an aortic dissection, got five more somewhat distant years and then lost him too. I helped raise my youngest sister, pretty much since she was a toddler. I learned the ropes of a family business and then I watched my grandfather lose his life's work. I packed up my childhood home. I buried my dog of 15 years.

In 2015, Matt totaled our car in an accident after a seizure. I didn't understand the severity until I arrived at the ER. That was the year he got the vagus nerve stimulator implanted—a small device that brought big hope. A quiet symbol of how we were still fighting for stability in a life that kept shifting underneath us.

And somewhere in the middle of all these layers of responsibility, I lost track of myself.

I kept showing up—at school drop-offs, meetings, OT, chiropractic care for the family, extracurriculars, dinner, the whole mental load and everything else in between that a high needs household needs because that's what we were. I brought stability. I worked to regulate nervous systems while still learning to regulate my own. But I was stuck in survival mode. Still bracing. Still waiting for the next emergency.

Matt still averaged one to three seizures a year, and by this point, many of them stemmed from missed medication. He was supposed to take it twice a day, and we had fallen into a routine of asking—every morning, every night.

"Did you take your meds?"

It became automatic. Necessary. But even with the reminders, there were lapses. Life got busy. Something got skipped. And the consequences were never small. The seizures came suddenly. Violently. And they left a ripple effect across all of us.

My nervous system wasn't the only one constantly on edge. I could also see it in the kids—in their bodies, their questions, the way they scanned my face for cues. Even in the quiet moments, we were always watching for the next storm.

At the time, I hadn't yet named the patterns I'd grown up in—the ways I had learned to anticipate moods, overfunction, tiptoe around instability, and carry more than was mine to carry. I didn't know then that I was living inside a pattern of codependence.

I hadn't realized that in marrying Matt, I had unknowingly chosen a dynamic that mirrored the one I knew: the instability of my childhood, my parents fighting, my mothers temperamental behavior, our complex relationship, and my father's drinking had all made my childhood unpredictable. Now, seizures shaped our rhythm the same way alcohol once had during my childhood.

But let me be clear: Matt was not the problem.

He was my rock.

He was one of the most stable, supportive forces in my life. He grounded me. We laughed together. We dreamed together. We built a life we were proud of. That's why I chose this song for us to dance to at our wedding, *Universe and U* by KY Tunstall. It said so much about how he showed up for me and grounded me after such an unstable path.

*"You cool me down when I'm cold inside / You are warm
and bright / You know you are so good for me..."*
*"We are just the same / And I can feel everything you do /
Hear everything you say—even when you're miles
away..."*

He loved me through so many dark chapters.

And still—his epilepsy shaped our home. It shaped our fears. It shaped our future. That's the thing no one talks about: How love and strain can live in the same house. How gratitude and exhaustion can sit at the same dinner table. How you can be holding someone up and falling apart at the same time.

By December 2016, we were more comfortable in the rhythms of early parenthood, more practiced in managing the daily demands.

But it came at a cost. A quiet toll was building. One I hadn't even noticed yet. I had gradually started drinking more—not every day, and not really before dinnertime. But a glass during the kids' bath time. Another after bedtime. A way to unwind. A way to exhale. A way to take the edge off. And the world I lived in made it feel justified. Alcohol was so normalized.

"Mommy needs wine"—printed on T-shirts and tea towels, wine glasses and memes. It seemed like soft permission.

But the truth is, drinking was a coping mechanism I had learned early in life—how to numb out the complexity, the heartbreak, the invisible weight of holding so much.

No one really tells you what it will take—what it costs—to be a mother.

No one tells you how heavy the mental load is.

How much you'll have to remember.

How little help you'll actually get.

How often you'll feel like you're drowning in tasks, worries, lunches, logistics, emotions—not just your own, but everyone else's too. No one tells you how much of yourself you'll lose. I couldn't even poop alone, much less read a book or make meaningful art. By that point, the only creative time I consistently carved out was once or twice a year—at craft weekends with other moms, women who often reserved this time for special projects, sometimes even for their kids' birthdays or holidays.

And then throw in the added complexity: I was afraid to leave my kids alone with Matt when they were young—not because he wasn't loving, but because I couldn't predict when a seizure might strike. It made my options feel even more limited. That's the real grief of motherhood that no one talks about:

The grief that lives in the early mornings and the late nights, the endless in-betweens. The grief of everything that quietly falls on the shoulders of moms.

Because dads—dads often get the playtime. The fun time.

And mothers? We struggle to play with our children at all, because we are damn near fully consumed with things like mom math—calculating what time we need to leave, when we will load up the car, what time we have to finish a report in order to leave to make it by school pickup, to what time dinner needs to be ready and how long it will take to prepare, and whether we can fit in a shower before the 6:00 p.m. school event. It's a constant quiet game of calculations to make sure we stay on schedule.

It's a whole science. And a work of art.

And the truth is—it robs mothers, especially working mothers, of some of the sweeter, easier moments we want with our kids. I loved those early days—when mine were younger, and we could go to parks and be in nature, and I could just watch them wander with wide eyes and wonder.

I loved witnessing their curiosity, their awe, their joy. But as they got older, those moments became fewer and farther between. There was more resistance. They didn't always want to follow anymore. The easy adventures became negotiations. And I missed the simplicity of those early years more than I knew how to say.

That morning I lost my job, after Matt had a seizure and I got the kids to school, I pulled into work like I had a hundred times before. I sat in that conference room and heard what was really being said: That in prioritizing my family, I had made choices that didn't align with the kind of time and availability the company expected from me.

They let me go in the same room that used to be my office. The one they expanded when I was pregnant. Not because I asked for it, but because they wanted to support me. A space where I could work and pump and breathe, where I could be both a professional and a mother.

There, in the room TW once reconfigured to honor my motherhood, they quietly ended my job. The very thing one business made *had* space for, another now counted against me.

I hadn't failed. But I had stepped outside their definition of success.

And for that, I was being unmistakably invited not to return.

I didn't cry. Not in the office.

I packed up my things and I left.

Not because I was strong—

but because I was already hollow.

What I didn't realize then was that this moment—this hemorrhage—would become its own kind of beginning. It would mark the end of a season where I had done everything right and still lost.

And it would begin the slow, painful work of asking: *What's next? Where will I go from here?*

And even now, I think back to that song—the one we danced to under twinkle lights, tulle and hope. When so much lay before us... We were always building something together.

Even when it hurt. Even when it cracked us open.

I didn't know it then, but the quiet I found in that season after losing my job wasn't peace—it was depletion. I spent the greater part of a year unraveling.

7

THE BONUS SUMMER
LOSING, LETTING GO, AND LISTENING

THE WINTER after I lost my job was one of fear and fog.

It wasn't just the absence of income—it was the absence of direction. Of identity. I'd gotten a severance package and then moved to unemployment benefits, something I had never utilized before. For the first time since I was fourteen, I wasn't working. I wasn't producing anything. As a firstborn daughter who'd spent her whole life measuring her worth by what she could manage, accomplish, or create—this was disorienting.

There was no roadmap for this in-between. No quick fix. No plan to pivot. Just long, quiet days and a mind full of noise.

It was a hard winter for my mental health.

I didn't know who I was without a job title. Without structure and routine. But slowly, something new started to stir.

It began with a conversation. A mom I'd grown close to at the kids' Montessori school was finishing her master's in social work and leading a support group for formerly homeless women. She told me something that stuck: that there was no women-only, daytime safe space in our city. And then she asked me a question that would quietly change the course of my life:

"Do you want to help me look into this?"
I didn't have much else going on.
I didn't have a plan.
But I knew a noble cause when I saw one.
And I said yes.

BY FEBRUARY, we had our first meeting. And something new was underway. Each referral led us to other people to connect with who confirmed there was indeed a need for a daytime safe space for women. So we kept connecting quietly, gaining new insights.

I spent some of my extra time volunteering at the kids' school, something I had been wanting to do. So, on Wednesdays, I joined other moms helping make learning materials for the Montessori classrooms. It gave me a chance to be involved in school and allowed me to keep taking them to the park with friends when school let out —that was a favorite of theirs and mine. While they played I formed new friendships on the playground. I loved the community I found at that school. At one point I think we were one of the only families from Louisville who attended, many of the families were transplants from other states, even from other countries. I loved the diversity it offered all of us.

The summer of 2017 brought a whole new wave of energy. There was so much change in the air—more than I could even see yet.

I perfected my frugality, stretching our dollars further than ever.

We brewed kombucha, harvested veggies from our garden, and turned science experiments into summer fun. We built forts, made art, played Jenga, took naps in the hammock, and exploded watermelons with rubber bands.

We explored waterfalls. Rode scooters. Took adventures in my convertible, exploring the local cultural pass through the library.

We even got a beach trip in with Matt's family and spent long, sun-warmed afternoons at the pool and parks. We spent time on the boat with Matt's family and filled our summer with more fun than

I'd ever gotten to share with the kids and I was humbled and grateful.

It was a gift.

A summer I wouldn't have had if I hadn't lost my job.

A summer that softened something in me.

A summer I was finally able to share with my children.

AT THE SAME TIME, we kept meeting with community members to keep us moving forward with the shelter and started working with a legal organization to figure out how to structure a nonprofit.

It was unstructured. Unfamiliar. Uncertain. And it was also expansive.

That summer was the first time I began to allow myself to unwind. Not just from the job I had lost—but from the pressure I had carried for decades. It was liberating. It was uncomfortable. It was a bonus season of motherhood and creativity I hadn't planned for, but maybe—just maybe—it was exactly what I needed.

Then, a family friend from the Montessori school, who had just completed a multi-year engineering project in the city, prepared to return to Europe. They offered us something unexpected for our cause: furniture and supplies. A lot of them. So we rented a U-Haul, a storage unit, and set off to secure our first donated assets: chairs, tables, bookshelves—things we would need to start a women's shelter.

We were on our way.

At the same time, I was networking—reaching out to partners, building relationships, listening to the community. We were conducting a needs assessment, meeting with women who would eventually become the heart of our mission, women who needed our services.

We interviewed more than forty women across partner agencies and visited local encampments with trusted community members. We wanted to learn directly from the people most impacted—what they needed, where they felt safe, what was missing.

We met them where they were.

And I began to understand just how much we take for granted.

One summer evening, we were visiting a homeless encampment when a woman shared her story with us. She had been living there for a while, and as we talked, she said something I'll never forget: "You smell so good. I miss smelling good."

It hit me like a punch to the chest. That small detail—so human, so overlooked. She shared it with such sadness and longing. Later that night, I got home and washed the sweat and heat of the day away. I put on my lotion, changed into pajamas, and sat with that moment. The sheer privilege of smelling clean, feeling safe, of tucking my children into bed with no fear of who might come to the door.

I was seeing the world through a new lens.

And I knew then—I couldn't unsee it.

I had to be part of the solution.

Over and over again, the women we met confirmed what we suspected: they needed a safe, women-only space. They told us stories of sleeping with box cutters in their bras. Of hiding in wooded areas, parking garages, or abandoned buildings to avoid predators. Of keeping their children out of shelters for fear of being separated by CPS.

Some found temporary help through family, but it often came with strings attached—dysfunction, instability, trauma repeating itself.

We listened.

To women navigating physical abuse, abandonment, substance use, mental illness, generational poverty. To stories from women who had no safe place to go. To young women aging out of foster care with nowhere to turn. To children caught in systems that mistook poverty for neglect. And we learned even more about a system seemingly designed to break them, not support them. We learned that the data on women was limited—and on children, even more so.

We partnered with a local domestic violence shelter to attend their onboarding trainings, learning how to build trauma-informed care into the foundation of what we were creating.

Everyone we met confirmed the need.

Everyone pointed us toward more connections.

Everyone said the same thing: keep going.

JUST BEFORE THE Fourth of July, I was outside on our deck during a quiet weekday afternoon. Matt came out after a meeting and said he needed to talk.

The look on his face told me everything. Something was wrong. Seriously wrong.

"I just lost my job," he said softly.

A wave of shock hit him first—and then crashed directly into the center of my chest. My heart skipped. I froze.

Keep breathing, I told myself.

But all I could think was: This can't be happening. It had been barely six months since I lost my job. We were already operating on half our income. And now this? This felt like too much.

What do we do?

When school started back up, I returned to business with the shelter project—because there was no other option. The nonprofit was gaining traction, and it was time to move. We filed our articles of incorporation. We officially became an organization. We formed our board of directors. We mailed out formal invitations for our first board meeting. Somehow, even in the midst of my personal uncertainty, things kept falling into place.

The stars aligned.

The momentum was unmistakable. It felt as if the universe had cleared the path for a shelter that women in our community desperately needed. And yet, I have little memory of how the rest of that day—or the first few days after Matt's job loss—really played out. I was operating in shock. One foot in front of the other. Auto-pilot.

Matt, meanwhile, was steady as usual.

He reassured me that we would be fine. He had a degree in computer information systems, an MBA, and a specialized background in IT—data mining, data engineering. The kind of expertise that made him valuable in highly technical roles, even if it sometimes kept him from pivoting toward the business analyst work he preferred. He told me recruiters reached out often. That he'd find something. That we'd figure it out.

I envied his calm.

I needed a plan B—always had.

Usually a plan C, too.

And with private school starting in less than six weeks, all I could think was: This is not sustainable.

"Hard not to worry" didn't even begin to cover it.

We were leveling up in a way we couldn't yet see.

"And just like stars burning bright/
Making holes in the night/We are building bridges."
—KT Tunstall, Universe & U

That line had lived in our wedding song, but I hadn't known just how true it would become. Even now, in the fear and the uncertainty, we were still building. Still burning through the dark. That energy matched everything happening in the sky at the time.

I felt like I carried the worry for both of us over the next four to six weeks. I'm sure Matt had some of his own—but he didn't show it. He stayed cool. Calm. Present. He took the kids to the pool. We spent more family time all together that summer than we ever had before. And even in my panic, I could feel the gift of it—the beauty of just being with one another in a way we'd never had the space for. As much as I could, I tried to stay present and focus on the hand we'd been dealt. But the planner and preparer in me couldn't help but spiral. I grew overly anxious in ways that I'm sure raised the temperature in our home. I brought my fear into the atmosphere. Still, I always admired how Matt handled that period of time. How calm he stayed. How he protected our peace.

Part of me worried he was holding all that anxiety inside to shield the rest of us. I prayed for him—his health, his mind, his heart. And yet, another part of me—the part that knew how smart, capable, and grounded he was—trusted he was right. We would figure it out. But this was different than the scrappy years. We weren't college kids who could survive on ramen and luck. We were a family of four, with private school tuition due in a couple of weeks. The stakes were so much higher.

In mid-August, Matt accepted a contract role with a large local organization. A wave of relief washed over our home. He was set to start on August 21, 2017—the day of the total solar eclipse.

The first in our lifetime that either of us would remember.

But what I didn't realize yet was that the stars were already moving in our favor. While I spent my days worrying, the universe was quietly rearranging everything. And on a day none of us would ever forget, the sky itself would offer a message I didn't know I needed to hear:

It's time.

WRITTEN IN THE STARS, ROOTED IN THE GROUND

That Sunday, as Matt prepared for his first day at a new job, I packed up the kids, the cooler, the snacks, and our camping gear. We were headed west into the path of totality, to witness something we might only see once in a lifetime: the total solar eclipse of 2017.

I didn't know it then, but I wasn't just chasing a cosmic event. I was walking straight into my own transformation.

The heat was already rising as we pulled into the field in Hopkinsville to meet my sister. Months earlier we had selected a point in the path with the most seconds in totality. Strangers smiled at one another like old friends. Music floated through the summer air. The buzz of excitement was almost too much to bear.

The countdown had begun.

The sweltering evening brought with it, a new magnetic energy. We set up camp, securing our spot next to a line of trees that provided some shade with excellent viewing for the eclipse. Then we went and explored the local town, taking photos while sharing our excitement for what the eclipse would bring the next day. More than 100 people were camping out in this field in the middle of nowhere, and the buzz was growing as the countdown drew closer.

We awoke the next morning to find food trucks, delightful music playing, lots of varieties of happy, spellbound hippies and star and sky enthusiasts, who were super electrified to watch the eclipse. The minutes melted away and heat rose like a tide. Layers of sweat covered our bodies and we could hardly stand the euphoric energy that was gradually overcoming us. My sister and I set up a time lapse video to capture this once in a lifetime scene. And as the new moon started to cross the path of the sun, we became increasingly mesmerized. It was exacerbated by the charged energy of the crowd which was similar to being at a concert and sharing such a unique experience with so many people who have such love for the same moment in time, it was purely magical.

As the sun began making its pilgrimage behind the moon, we heard the cows begin to moo a rooster crow. The crickets started chirping, and the sky grew as dark as dusk. It was absolutely incredible and I've never seen or felt anything like it. I can tell you I felt the shift, it took my breath away.

They say eclipses bring great energy for change and growth, beginnings and new opportunities and that's exactly what it was doing for us. It was showing my family there was a new way, it was showing my husband a new job opportunity, and the shelter plan I was working on kept unfolding at an expedited rate. Change was certainly in the air for all of us and the heightened energy felt electric.

I rode that awestruck feeling for days, it was truly enchanting. My whole meaning was altered and I was mesmerized by that beautiful photographic freeze frame image of the moon total eclipse in the sun. I kept listening to Pink Floyd's "Dark Side of the Moon" and got really philosophical. I listened to more music than I had in a long time. I thought about my dad and how I would have loved to have viewed the eclipse with him. There was a new sense of depth to life and purpose that I couldn't quite put my finger on, but I could feel it. I was transformed with this visceral knowing that something in me had shifted and I would never be the same.

I was called into something greater and immediately started looking up when the next eclipses would be happening. I knew that there was no way I would miss the one in 2024. It was like I had been given a new big dose of lifeforce energy. I was recharged and ready to conquer anything, to live my best life. And that's exactly what I started to do.

August 2017 marked a profound turning point both personally and collectively, ignited by the Great American Eclipse in Leo. The world was called to shed what no longer served and to remember what had always been true. It opened a new seven-year cycle centered around self-expression, leadership, and authentic living. For me, someone deeply rooted in nurturing energies, the eclipse demanded a shift, moving me away from emotional caretaking and into bold, unapologetic creation. It was a season of reclaiming personal power, stepping into visibility, and leading from the heart.

Some moments aren't just written in time; they are etched into the soul and the summer of 2017 was one of them.

The seeds planted that August would grow into UP, a living embodiment of the leadership, authenticity, and heart-centered vision this era called forth. I moved forward with a "who's going to stop us" energy, mostly, I think, to keep my own fear at bay because failure wasn't an option.

That resolve only deepened when voices long buried rose to the surface in October 2017, as the #MeToo movement (first sparked years earlier by activist Tarana Burke) erupted into public awareness, shaking the foundations of silence and shame.

UP wasn't formed in isolation; it rose within this charged atmosphere. In August, we finalized our Articles of Incorporation, filed for 501(c)(3) status, assembled our first Board of Directors, and deepened partnerships with organizations already building change. We weren't riding the wave; we were part of the wave. UP was not a reaction; it was a calling answered. It carried the pulse of a new era: one where authenticity, courage, and collective power would no longer be hidden but honored, cultivated, and unleashed. The same cosmic forces that tore open the old were the ones breathing life into what we dared to imagine next.

THE DOORS OPENED
A SEASON OF STRETCHING

Five months after filing our initial paperwork, in January 2018, our nonprofit determination letter arrived, validating our 501(c)(3) status and pushing us forward with new momentum.

At the same time, we were laying the groundwork to get our doors open. All of the city funding was reimbursement-based, so we needed cash-in-hand to launch. By that spring, somewhere near $48,000 was awarded by the city, giving us a much-needed foundation to build on. Shortly after, Women4Women Foundation awarded us a $25,000 grant, the final piece we needed to open. Around the same time, we found a partnership in Christ Church Cathedral, a perfect location in the heart of downtown Louisville, right along the bus line, where space often sat empty during the week. Everything was finally clicking into place.

On July 16, 2018, UP for Women and Children opened our doors to the community for the very first time, welcoming six women that day. TW was one of our first shelter volunteers and welcomed the women as they arrived. Just weeks later, we hosted the mayor, our District 4 Councilwoman, a representative from our congressman's office, and local partners as we cut the ribbon in the basement of the

Diocesan House of Christ Church Cathedral. It was truly a special moment: a testament to the grit, faith, and collaboration it had taken to get us there. And just like that, we were officially up and running.

It didn't take long for the need for our services to become clear. In that first year, we welcomed more than 400 unique individuals. That winter, we pitched to a local foundation (a process that felt a little like nonprofit Shark Tank) and secured the funding we needed to grow. By the fall of 2019, we were ready to bring on a second practicum student and an additional AmeriCorps member, expanding our small but mighty team to eight. We were growing steadily in our tiny basement startup space, laying the foundation for everything that would come next.

There are seasons in life when you know you are standing at a threshold. You can feel it in your bones, the quiet certainty that you are no longer who you once were, even if the world hasn't quite caught up yet. That was the season I found myself in.

One of the greatest lessons I learned on this journey is this: You cannot do it alone. Great support will make or break you. It is so important to surround yourself with the right people: the ones who will have your back, who will remind you of the hard truths, who will challenge you to be better, who will guide you away from mistakes and help you get out of your own way.

I needed all kinds of people along the road: support from other local leaders, dedicated board members, brilliant staff, remarkable colleagues, amazing mentors, and fabulous friends. And I was lucky. When you give your time and heart to something that impacts the community in a meaningful way, people *want* to help you. They want to see you succeed, especially once they understand the magnitude of the work you're leading.

Sara Blakely, the founder of Spanx, philanthropist and a Forbes billionaire, once said that one of her greatest blessings was her circle of fellow entrepreneurs, people she could brainstorm with, seek guidance from, and vent to when needed. I understand that now more than ever.

Because the wrong people (the naysayers, the critics, the complainers) will poke holes in your ideas simply because it's easier than building something themselves. You have to find the people who will lift you up, encourage you, inspire you, push you, and challenge you to become who you're meant to be.

I'm forever grateful for the people who chose to believe in me, who coached and mentored me during that time, and who connected me with even more good people along the way. One of the best pieces of advice an early mentor gave me was simple: "Every time you meet with someone, ask them to recommend two more people you should talk to."

It was simple yet brilliant advice and also harder for me to execute than it might have been for others. Small talk has never come naturally to me, it's something I have really had to work at. I've always been drawn to the deep end of conversation, to the questions that touch the soul, the purpose, the "why" behind everything we do.

HOLDING TWO TRUTHS

Building authentic connections on behalf of the organization took extra energy, more intention, and a lot of heart. But every time I stretched myself to do it, it paid off in ways I couldn't have imagined.

That single habit expanded my network in ways I could have never predicted. Along the way, I was shown something I already knew in a new way: Those who have suffered, who have lost, who have been broken and stitched themselves back together, they often become the kindest, most generous people you will ever meet. It's because they know what pain feels like. And they know what healing requires. I had the honor of meeting many of them in our shelter.

Still, even with support near me, there were countless days that stretched me to my breaking point. The reality is, throughout this journey, I was fortunate to have access to a wide range of incredible people: provider partners (mostly healers and helpers), community leaders, government partners, other CEOs, volunteers, funders and of course, the women we served.

Those connections were one of the greatest gifts of my shift from the corporate world into nonprofit work. I met extraordinary people who poured their hearts into this mission, and I'm forever grateful for their partnership and support. But even with a strong network around me, leadership often carried a quiet kind of solitude. Especially for someone wired the way I am, drawn to depth and meaning over surface connection, it sometimes felt like I was moving through the world just a little differently.

I held both realities at once: deep gratitude for the people who showed up—and an understanding that the path I was walking would sometimes feel lonely simply because of the way I was built. There was so much back-and-forth in my role. So many days filled with fear, exhaustion, and uncertainty. In the early days, we were a small team serving between 50 and 90 women each day. The staff was often overwhelmed, we were mostly understaffed and still evolving. No one wanted to turn anyone away.

That decision was always collective. The team would tell me what they could manage, and I trusted them. Looking back, I might have drawn firmer boundaries to protect them. But at the time, they were clear: they wanted to serve. Even if it meant working at a pace that stretched them thin. The best people always seemed to find their way to UP. Their gifts were undeniable. We had former state employees, a chef, reiki practitioners, a published author and TEDx speaker, an engineer, a producer, another nonprofit founder, talented artists, a former client turned fashion designer, and a practicum student who later became an award-winning middle school counselor. They worked for less than they deserved, not because the work was easy, but because they believed in it. They believed in the women we served, and in the difference we were making on some of the darkest days of their lives. We all took that responsibility seriously.

So I made it a strategic priority to pay people a living wage. Every year, I worked to raise the base pay, which always meant finding more funding. It meant expanding the team, securing stronger benefits, celebrating birthdays and anniversaries, buying lunch, and investing in our people however we could.

Still, the hard part remained: most of our team were direct

service staff, because that's what funders wanted to support. But nonprofits are businesses—100%. And like any business, we needed infrastructure. Administrative support. Systems. Capacity. We were building a foundation that would last and we strived to do everything the right way.

As I stepped from founder to CEO, my responsibilities shifted. I had to increase visibility, manage HR, oversee operations, support the team, and still often jump in to cover shelter shifts. I could go from pulling a used syringe out of the trash can, to calling 911, to giving a donor a tour, to gathering supplies for a guest or helping them with laundry. However I was needed, I showed up. There was nothing in that building I'd ask someone to do that I hadn't already done myself.

So the shift, recognizing that I needed to step back from those day-to-day roles so I could be strategic, represent us in the community, and keep elevating our work, was challenging. It was hard because I wanted to stay relatable to the team. I wanted them to know I had their back.

Some days, it all just felt like too much. On those days, I would take a hike, go to bed early, cry if I needed to, and wake up determined to find new inspiration again.

It was a constant process of recalibration: picking myself up off the floor, reminding myself how far we had come, and pushing forward toward the future I could feel but not always see. It was a lesson in trust. Keep showing up, putting one foot in front of the other, doing the next right thing. The stakes kept getting higher.

There were more paychecks to meet, more capital to raise, more women and children depending on us as our numbers climbed sharply and dramatically. When the pressure mounted, I always came back to the heart of it: The stories. The women. The people we served. Their stories kept me tethered to our mission when the leadership demands: the HR policies, the budgets, the grant deadlines, the operational reserves—threatened to pull me into pure business survival mode. But the truth was, leading people in this work is never just about operations or compliance. It's human.

In a human services organization, people are both the heartbeat and the heartbreak. Many of our staff carried their own history of trauma, even as they showed up every day to help others heal. Supporting and protecting the team wasn't just good leadership, it was a sacred responsibility. Because when your mission is built on human resilience, caring for the people doing the work is as vital as caring for the people you serve. The health of the mission depended on it.

And, we were a business. We had to stay out of deficit. We had to build a reserve fund and emergency safeguards to survive. But at the center of all of it were human beings—real women, real lives, real futures. Many of the women we served carried unbearable trauma. They had been assaulted, raped, trafficked, locked away without escape, stripped of their dignity and hope. I heard story after story that made me want to scream at a world that could fail people so completely.

Some women woke up naked next to dumpsters. Some stopped reporting their assaults to police because they knew nothing would come of it and that reliving their trauma would only be met with disbelief or indifference. I remember one shift in particular, going with a woman to a SANE exam (Sexual Assault Nurse Examiner exam) at a local hospital. These exams are invasive, exhausting, retraumatizing. They involve head-to-toe physical exams, genital exams, collection of bodily fluids, hair, skin, clothing—every possible scrap of evidence, documented and photographed.

It is a brutal process.

And I was horrified when they assigned a male nurse to conduct her exam. He walked into the room without a trace of compassion, dropped paper gowns on the changing table, and told her to change without even leaving the room. She looked so small. So scared. I asked her quietly if she wanted a woman instead. She nodded yes.

We requested a female nurse, and I gently told him that she would prefer privacy while changing.

The exam took hours.

I waited outside the room, a quiet support in a system that seemed determined to break her all over again. Afterward, we grabbed some food, and I drove her back to the shelter where she was staying. She thanked me for coming with her. I thanked her for trusting me. I drove home that night heartbroken that these were still the choices women faced. That this was still the best the system could offer.

8

THE WORLD BEGAN TO SHIFT

AS WINTER MELTED INTO SPRING, news of a novel coronavirus began to swirl in the background, quiet at first, but growing louder by the day. At first, it seemed scary but far away. Until it wasn't.

On Friday, March 13, 2020, everything changed. It was the last day my daughter attended her school in person (fifth grade) and by Monday, virtual learning platforms were built almost overnight.

At UP, we moved our services to a larger first-floor space to allow for social distancing. The warm, living room-like atmosphere of our original small basement space gave way to a sterile room with chairs spaced six feet apart. We wore masks. We sanitized constantly. We adapted on the fly. And within days, our team of eight had shrunk to a team of three.

Our practicum students had been pulled from their sites. Ameri-Corps members lost childcare and couldn't return. Another team member had health vulnerabilities and could no longer work onsite. It became three of us, holding the line. When indoor services became unsafe, we took to the courtyard, distributing mail, food, supplies, and encouragement under the open sky. Even in the darkest moments, we remained a beacon of hope, a friendly, familiar face in the chaos. We didn't have a playbook. We just had each other. And we kept going.

THE SUMMER OF UNKNOWING

The summer of 2020 was a season of heartbreak, hope, and a powerful demand for justice, felt in every corner of downtown Louisville and beyond.

Living and working in the heart of Louisville changed after the killing of Breonna Taylor, who died during the execution of a no-knock warrant. In the weeks and months that followed, peaceful protests took place, calling for justice in her name. From my vantage point downtown, the events portrayed in some media outlets differed from what I saw firsthand—coverage that, in my view, kept many people away from the city's center. I knew business owners who had clients who were scared to come downtown, meanwhile it was eerily quiet on our street.

It was the boarded-up windows of the Omni Hotel across from our shelter. It was the protests filling Jefferson Square Park, voices raised in grief and defiant hope. It was the soul-deep, unavoidable call for change that reverberated through the streets and into every breath we took.

At UP, we bore witness to the injustices firsthand, through the experiences of our clients, through our own advocacy, and eventually through the stories we shared with the Department of Justice's investigation into the Louisville Metro Police Department. Many of the women we served had experienced harmful or dismissive treatment by law enforcement, and we knew their voices were often overlooked.

I'll never forget the time we had to call the police for a woman with a Mental Inquest Warrant (MIW), one we had filed ourselves for her protection. It was delicate. We had worked hard to build rapport and trust with her. When the officers arrived, she was calm, cooperative, and genuinely trying to do the right thing. It was truly best case scenario. As they prepared to escort her out, she asked if she could smoke a cigarette. One of the officers replied, "As long as you're not acting crazy."

I wasn't exactly surprised—but I was furious. It was the kind of careless, dehumanizing response that reveals just how deeply systems fail people with mental health needs. How could professionals responding to mental health-related calls so blatantly lack trauma-informed training or compassion? It was baffling and deeply telling. In a way, I was both surprised and not surprised at all.

Then there was the time we waited over two hours for a response to a 911 call. Two hours. That was the moment it hit us: no one was coming. Not in any kind of timely fashion. If we were going to keep our team and our clients safe, we were going to have to figure it out ourselves. That realization ushered in a new layer of responsibility— one we hadn't trained for, and one that became significantly harder to navigate in the aftermath of COVID, when so many in-person trainings disappeared overnight. Virtual options slowly began to emerge, but we needed tools and knowledge immediately. Something to ground us, protect us, and empower us in the absence of timely outside help.

And still, there were also many moments of great care. We had some truly positive experiences with LMPD officers as well. Both were true. There were times when officers showed compassion, patience, respect—and went above the call of duty. Which only underscored the larger truth: we *can* do better. Not through more money for jails or punitive systems, but through real investments in education, training, and trauma-informed, preventative support. That's what makes safer communities—for everyone.

And even as the world outside cried out for justice, I carried another, quieter awakening within myself.

I didn't know the first day I masked.

I didn't know the first day I hid the parts of me that didn't fit into a world built for someone else.

But that summer, standing at the intersection of collective grief and personal truth, I began to feel it:

I could not keep hiding.

Not from the world.

Not from myself.

THE WINTER I DIDN'T SEE COMING

The holiday season of 2020 was strange for everyone. That Christmas Day we drove out to the farm to take TW and Sonny some homemade cookies. We weren't going in, we didn't want to take any chances in case we somehow unknowingly had COVID, but TW always appreciated homemade food and goodies. So we loaded up and headed to the country. We rang the bell and delivered the cookies. I had TW take a selfie with me from the doorway to capture our Christmas visit. I told him I loved him and to let us know if they needed anything. He thanked us for coming.

As I stepped away from the porch, I was intuitively called to roam the grounds a bit with my family. I know it sounds crazy but suddenly a jolt of electricity buzzing up directly from the Earth and through my body. I received a message, and it was very clear: this would be TW's last Christmas.

We visited an old tree I loved, one we'd passed by for decades and played alongside as kids. We walked around and I admired the landscape. I took it all in like it somehow might be my last visit with him residing there, the sanctuary of my childhood, swinging in the tree and the pond we used to sit and admire, the one TW would fish in. So we took pictures of us and of the land.

This was my first home. And there, beside the tree we'd spent decades swinging under, my roots—quite literally—sent me a message. I could feel the weight of an era that was ending. It was heavy and caught me by surprise, but I was so thankful for the heads up. Grateful for the gift of reflection, for of all the memories and blessings and having my family there beside me. It gave me the chance to take pictures, to take it all in, before life as I knew it slipped away.

Over the next few months, TW was navigating health issues and was scheduled to get a heart ablation. The hospital was only a few blocks from the shelter, so I could easily stop by midday or on my way to or from work to check on him.

On one of visit, just as I was leaving his room, I heard him tell the nurse "That's my granddaughter," his voice full of pride. I could hear the smile in it, and that meant everything. By then, I would tease him and say things like "Did you ever think you would have a silver-haired granddaughter" and we'd chuckle.

They released him, but before a week had passed, Sonny called. She was concerned, my grandfather was not doing well. This time he wanted to go to a different hospital, one he knew better, so my uncle took him. They admitted him, and while there, he caught COVID from his roommate. This time, they wouldn't let me see him. Because of restrictions, the ICU wasn't allowing visitors. He declined quickly, was put on a ventilator, then started slipping out of touch with reality.

I went to the hospital. I begged them to let me be with him, said it wasn't right, that no one should spend their final days alone. They wouldn't budge. I explained I understood the risks, I could get COVID, fine whatever, I would sign a waiver. I would have signed anything to be there with him. He'd done so much for me, so much for many, it just wasn't right. And although my uncle assured me he was no longer really there and wouldn't know if we were there, I knew and he still deserved some company.

In a loss almost as traumatic as my mother's, TW left this Earth at the age of 88. From that cold, sterile hospital in our first COVID winter, my grandfather slipped away alone. I was beyond devastated. Even now, the loss knocks the breath from me. I feel it in my chest, my heart aching for his big 'ole heart. He'd had an extraordinary run, a legacy worth marveling over. He was an incredible storyteller, the best.

At the funeral, Sonny, who hadn't seen him in a few weeks either due the hospital restrictions, made her way over to the casket.

She cried out "He was my best friend" and nearly collapsed if not for my uncle holding her up. Her heartbreak rippled through all of us.

People joke about getting older; I have, too. I've laughed about things that start happening in your forties that I thought wouldn't come until my sixties. But the truth is, getting older is a privilege not afforded to all. I've seen that first hand. I don't ever want to take it for granted.

I like to think that, while TW was physically alone in that room, he wasn't alone in the crossing—he had so many beautiful people on the other side waiting to welcome him. He'd lost a lot of amazing people.

Memories of decades on the farm flashed through my mind. It was heart wrenching but there we were, sharing the beautiful life they had built, laughing at the pranks my grandfather had pulled. I even heard a few new stories I'd never known. I treasured every one of them, just as I did him. He had been like a second father to me, especially after losing my parents young. It's hard to put into words the role he played in my life. Now I carry him with me. Always.

A NEW KIND OF JOURNEY

In the wake of all that heartbreak and reckoning, I found myself quietly building a new kind of strength, one rooted not in control, but in courage. As the world slowly reopened, I realized I didn't want to return to the life I had before. I didn't want to live small, afraid, or confined by old narratives that no longer fit. I wanted to live awake. I wanted to live unmasked. I wanted to live wide open, even when it scared me.

In the still winter months of 2021, tucked into the quiet of January and February, I began dreaming from the comforts of my bathtub not of survival, but of possibility. I spent hours planning, researching, and daring to believe that something extraordinary could be within reach for my family.

And so that summer, when the world still felt uncertain and my own footing still felt new and shaky, I packed up our SUV with camping supplies, homemade activity binders for the 5,000 mile journey that lay before us, loaded my family inside, and set out for Yellowstone, Grand Teton, Glacier, and the Badlands. With Glacier alone being a thirty-hour journey from home.

Grand Teton stole my heart, it was majestic and breathtaking.

Yellowstone reminded me of the vast beauty of our country with its extraordinary landscape and stunning wildlife from bison to wolves. There were many unforgettable stops along the way, each one stretching something inside of me, reminding me that wonder was still possible even after so much loss.

But Glacier...Glacier was the crown jewel, the destination my heart had set its sights on from the very beginning. I had prepared my kids for an 8 mile hike to Grinnell Glacier where we would pass the gorgeous, iconic Grinnell Lake that would leave me chasing alpine lakes for years to come.

We arrived in Glacier National Park just in time for the summer solstice, the longest day of the year and two days later, my birthday. I was in heaven. Standing there, surrounded by breathtaking mountains, towering cedar and evergreen trees and endless sky, I felt elated, overwhelmed, grateful, and so damn proud.

Proud that we had made it. Proud that I had dared to believe in this wild adventure. Proud that even after all the heartbreak, I still knew how to chase joy and show my children that anything is possible.

We hiked the eight mile out and back to Grinnell lake, pushing ourselves beyond easy comfort, fueled by trail mix, affirmations and pure wonder. We weren't able to fully make it because there was still snow and ice on the trail. We didn't have crampons and I knew the right choice was to turn back but it didn't matter because we had already done it.

Did I mention we even passed a grizzly bear on our way back down? A mere 50 feet from the trail. It was hard to believe: a little scary, a lot of awe, and I was incredibly grateful to see it from a safe distance as it slowly meandered away from us. Because I really did not want to have to use that bear spray.

I remember taking a photo of myself at the end of that hike, beaming with a pride that couldn't be contained. It wasn't just the mountain I had climbed, it was everything else, too.

All the fear, the grief, the self-doubt. I had carried it all up that mountain and left a piece of it behind in the snowmelt.

Anything felt possible again.

And for the first time in a long time, I believed it.

That trip didn't erase the hard parts. Matt still had seizures. I still carried the weight of preparedness. But something shifted in me. I stopped waiting for life to feel stable before I allowed myself to live it.

Caregiving taught me to be hyper-vigilant, always bracing for the next emergency, the next call, the next fall. But on that trip, in the long, slow return to ourselves, I started learning how to live alongside the unknown rather than in fear of it.

I spent years trying to control every variable, every outcome. And yet, the real strength was in the surrender. The resilience wasn't built by knowing everything would be okay, it was built by learning to move forward anyway. By loving through uncertainty. By choosing joy and wonder, even when the ground still felt shaky, often *especially* when the ground still felt shaky.

That journey taught me that living wide open doesn't mean you aren't scared.

It means you keep going.

You keep putting one foot in front of the other, with your fear, your grief, your love, your courage. All of it.

9

THE COST OF CARRYING IT ALL

BY JULY 2023, I was honored and honestly amazed to celebrate five years of UP. It was a milestone that meant everything to me. I had learned early on that 80% of nonprofits fail within the first five years, and I was determined to be part of the 20% that made it. That day wasn't just a celebration, it was a declaration: *we were still standing, still serving, and stronger than ever.* I was truly on cloud nine.

We marked the occasion with warmth, gratitude, and intention. A local grocer sponsored lunch for our guests, one of our partner churches served ice cream and cake, and for the first time ever, we opened our doors to the public. We had never done that during operations before, out of respect for the privacy and safety of those we serve. But this was a one-time celebration, and it felt important to let people see what we built.

The mayor and local council representatives, as well as several state representatives, attended, along with funders, supporters, and community members who had taken an interest in our work. It was a huge success. More than 60 people toured the space that day.

We connected with a new board member with expertise in fundraising and sponsorships. She was a real force and a true gift.

She arrived at our door in a crisp dress and bright lipstick, exuding the kind of confident energy that made you sit up straighter. Her eyes lit up as we spoke about the mission, and she leaned in, already imagining the possibilities. Within minutes, she was asking smart, strategic questions and tossing out sponsorship ideas like she'd been with us for years. It felt like we hadn't just met a board member, we'd been handed a spark.

We also met a new funder who happened to stop by, saw our work in action, and later awarded us a five-figure grant to support our children's programming. They have been an annual supporter since. Neither meeting was planned, but both felt divinely timed.

Our clients were excited to celebrate with us, grateful for the delicious lunch and spirit of joy we carried that day. Several women proudly shared pieces of their stories with attendees. How we had helped them on their journeys and how grateful they were for our safe space. Volunteers proudly led tours, sharing behind-the-scenes experiences of how they made a real difference every shift. Even my husband jumped in and gave an impromptu tour because, as the attendees kept arriving, we needed more tour guides. People were excited and amazed to see all the good work that was going on behind the scenes at UP. They were shocked by the number of women and children using our services. Many said they "had no idea" how many folks were in desperate need of services. We had built something powerful from scratch and as I stood there taking it all in, I couldn't help but feel proud. The room felt it too.

But as the excitement of that moment faded, the stakes only continued to grow. The work didn't slow down. If anything, it accelerated.

I was approaching burnout, not just from work, but from life. It was everything at once. Perimenopause, lack of quiet space to recharge and be my best self, the relentless demands of parenting during its busiest season, the constant effort to meet the individual needs of my children, and the unending work of managing a household while leading a grassroots startup nonprofit that, by its seventh year, had grown into a seven-figure operation.

With every passing year, our expenses increased, which meant it was up to me to grow the revenue to sustain it. We were now a team of sixteen, with four contract consultants. Twenty people depended on UP for their paychecks. Ensuring we could cover payroll, including annual raises, became one of my highest priorities. We had to pay people a living wage. Meanwhile, the number of women and children we were serving surged to an all-time high.

At home, I often felt at the mercy of the shifting emotional tides of middle and high schoolers. I'd worked so hard to create a safe, open environment that some days, I felt more like a doormat, flattened under the weight everyone else needed to unload. The school commute was a time that became an emotional pressure valve for our household, mornings could be tense. One child mentally geared up for a day of masking and overstimulation, while the other gravitated to their phone, which I tried to keep at bay to preserve a little connection and calm. The afternoon car ride became the space where it all spilled out: frustration, exhaustion, recess conflicts, bullying, silence, or sometimes a sharp comment aimed in my direction. Not because I had done anything wrong, but because I was the safest place to land. This often came at the expense of the other child, who was routinely more cheerful after school and ready to share about their day.

Parenting two very different kids meant constantly navigating polarity, one needing quiet and space, the other craving connection and conversation. Their needs often stood in contrast, and meeting them both required ongoing recalibration, negotiation, and deep attunement. It kept me on my toes, and it wasn't easy. But the same tools I was honing in my personal and professional development (emotional regulation, deep listening, boundary-setting, and repair) were the very ones that helped me level up as a parent. It wasn't about perfection. It was about presence.

As a parent, that's a hard place to live. I was navigating my own stress, often depleted from a full day myself. But I kept reminding myself not to take it personally. To be the person I needed at that age. Someone who could hold the weight without collapsing under it. Some days I managed it with grace. Other days, I didn't. But I always tried to lead with love.

And still, I was grateful to have created that space. I kept reminding myself to be the person I needed at that age.

But middle school and teenage parenting is not for the faint of heart. One moment, you're adored. The next, you're resented or feeling resentful. The shift can happen without warning. And while I knew it wasn't personal (it was developmental), that didn't make it hurt any less or feel easier to hold.

And the icing on the cake is that when your kids start having periods, you are working your way out of yours. Quietly, under the radar, with side effects no one told you about.

Perimenopause brought a kind of fog I hadn't expected, one that settled in my brain and made thinking feel slower, heavier, and more strained. On the good days, my thoughts came easily. But, on many others, even basic decisions felt like climbing uphill. I'd forget names of people I saw somewhat regularly, misplace my phone while it was in my hand, or walk into a room and forget why I was there. It was like having senior moments in my 40s, only no one warned me they might start this early. That's the hardest part, really. No one tells you how sneaky and disorienting this phase can be until you're in it, blinking through the brain fog and wondering if you're just tired...or actually losing your mind.

Hot flashes hit at random, making my body feel like a furnace from the inside out. And heart palpitations had me driving to the hospital on more than one occasion thinking I was having a heart attack. On one of these visits I learned I was having a menopausal migraine... WT actual F? And more than anything, I craved quiet, a space to be alone, uninterrupted, just to catch my breath.

But space was hard to come by. We were deep in the thick of parenting: sports, school projects, social plans, extracurriculars, emotional check-ins. It wasn't the kids themselves; it was the pace of it all. And since teenagers aren't known for advance notice or calendar coordination, life felt like a constant reworking of the schedule. As the owner of the schedule and someone who thrives on structure, the endless adjustments left me feeling disoriented and worn down.

To reclaim the quiet I needed to function, and honestly, to stay well, other things had to give. Household responsibilities started slipping through the cracks. I found myself depending more and more on my husband to carry the weight at home, and thankfully, he stepped up and leaned in. It felt like his turn, and he met the moment with grace.

Thankfully, I'd already been gifted a partner who shared in the responsibilities of home and family. But like many women, I had carried more of the invisible load over the years, even while working full-time and leading at a high level. This season brought a much needed shift. He leaned in, not just to carry the load, but to carry more of it gracefully, steadily, and without hesitation. I had done the same in other seasons, and now it was his turn. And I was deeply, genuinely grateful.

In truth, I wouldn't be where I am today with UP, with this book, with any of it—without his quiet, consistent dedication and support. It's something I don't take lightly. It's one of the greatest blessings of this entire journey.

This wasn't about resenting my family. It was about the sheer volume of need in every direction: my body's shifting needs, my mind's craving for rest, the relentless pace of a busy household, and the emotional load of parenting through a complex season of life. I was approaching burnout not just from work, but from life. It was everything, all at once.

And just when I started to feel like my flame was fading, that I was barely holding onto the spark of myself, I met with a functional hormone specialist who, quite honestly, saved my life. She listened, ran labs, adrenal and genetic tests, explained what was happening in my body, and gave me a plan: a cortisol manager, a mix of supplements and hormone replacement therapy. Within weeks, I felt better than I had in years. More grounded. More present. More me. There is hope, and there is help but most women don't know where to look or who to ask or sometimes know that it is even related to menopause. I want them to know: you're not broken. You're not losing it. There's a way through.

Through my own healing and growth work, I'd learned a lot about boundaries, especially how long I had gone without them, thanks to my deeply wired inner people pleaser. I'd practiced. Strengthened. Fine-tuned. I could now set clear boundaries in newer relationships, in professional settings, and with increasing ease at work. But the boundaries closest to home? Those were the hardest. The oldest relationships: my husband, my siblings, my children. That's where the stakes felt highest. Those required more courage, more strength, more practice. Sometimes even scripts.

This is the reality of my life. And why, as a mom and a CEO, I often feel like I'm always on. Between lacking a village of elder support from my own side of the family, managing epilepsy care, being the primary driver in a household of teenagers, and carrying the invisible mental load, there was never really a pause. As the CEO, I carry the weight of every major decision at work. Not because I make them all, my role is usually to support those who do, but because, ultimately, I am accountable. That accountability can be heavy.

I'm incredibly grateful for the help we do have. My father-in-law, Matt's great aunt, and his mom (especially in the earlier years) have each played a role in helping us stay afloat: offering rides, presence, and practical support when it was needed most. They've been a lifeline during some of the most demanding seasons of parenting and work.

Still, on top of it all, I was navigating meal planning, school schedules, sports uniforms, ever-changing shoe sizes, and the never-ending growth of children who always seemed to need something.

In a household navigating sensory processing differences, even clothing could become its own mountain. Tags, sock seams, pants that were too stiff or too tight or the wrong kind of elastic or cuffed, collars that scratched, buttons that felt wrong, sweaters that were too itchy...finding something that worked was hard enough. Finding it again in the next size up a few months later felt like an impossible scavenger hunt.

It was the most challenging when they were growing into new sizes multiple times per year with very limited specific requirements. My kids would rather their clothes fit too tight than to be too wiggly, so I braced myself every season it was time to move up to the next size because the clothes would be more loose which meant we had to shift between brands. So I was either repeatedly in stores feeling constantly overstimulated trying to find the right clothing or shopping online to present a whole spread of possibilities of options while secretly praying something worked. It was excruciating for all of us. And then there was the returns process of all remaining items that didn't work across six stores, UGH.

If my children ever read this, I hope they know there was never a day I didn't love them with my whole heart. Both things are true.

I would do anything for them. Nothing about this reflection is about regret or blame. It's about raw, honest truth. And the truth is that motherhood is an incredibly complex, beautiful, exhausting, sacred thing and no one tells you enough about what to expect, or how much of yourself you'll have to exchange for it when you dive all in. Loving them deeply and feeling stretched thin were never in conflict; they were often happening at the very same time.

This is the story of how I carried it all, including them, and still found my way back to myself.

The most beautiful things we build—our families, our missions, our legacies—sometimes come at the cost of forgetting ourselves.

THE INVISIBLE LOAD

Beneath it all, there was the mental load, the constant, invisible weight of remembering, managing, and tending to every detail for everyone else. Part of my journey was realizing that if I wanted to keep building anything that mattered, I had to start weaving more care for myself into the fabric of my life, not just the scraps I managed to salvage during my earliest years of motherhood.

Sometimes, it felt like too much.

I'd think to myself: I would never actually *drive my van into the river...* but I understood how it could happen. Women can feel so alone, so overwhelmed in this work of mothering that sometimes it becomes unbearable, especially when we're under-rested, underfed, and stretched to the edges of our capacity, pouring ourselves into everyone else with nothing left in reserve.

Being a mother is the most important, incredible, awe-inspiring thing I will ever do. And it is also the hardest, especially when you care so deeply about getting it right.

It became imperative that I care for myself, too.

I hadn't always had the tools, the people, or the financial means to do so. But in recent years, I'd been deliberately prioritizing it more.

THE SLOW RETURN

During the pandemic, I began incorporating regular massage into my life, a nonnegotiable for releasing the stress that came from working through such an unprecedented time. What began as physical relief slowly revealed itself as something more: a way to release long-held trauma I hadn't even realized I was carrying until I started living a life without alcohol.

Because when you stop numbing out, when you stop reaching for that glass of wine to take the edge off, you begin to feel everything. All the time. Sometimes all at once. It is an exhausting, unfiltered process.

What I didn't know then was just how important massage and self-care would become in my healing. Thankfully, I had a wine budget to reallocate. Making that change remains one of the greatest gifts I've ever given myself, a gift of healing that continues to serve me better than anything I left behind.

Meanwhile, I'd also lowered my standards of what a "clean house" looked like. I was not managing the finely manicured home of my childhood. Ours was often messy or what I liked to call "lived in." Unmade beds, stacks of books, curiosity-sparking materials, and art supplies were part of the landscape. It wasn't always orderly. With kids, things are constantly being passed on, and you have to decide what to bring in even when you're still trying to get things out. No matter how much we donated or simplified, it always felt like too much.

My kids got good at it, though. They cleaned out their rooms and closets unprompted whenever clothes got too small or too worn. It was wonderful, until I realized I had become responsible for getting it all out of the house. If only I could say the same for my own closet and the endless list of items that no longer suited us.

I never really prioritized it, because honestly, I was usually driving someone somewhere, investing in quality time, carving out creative space, exercising or, dare I say it... resting. Laying on my deck couch or hammock and reading became one of my favorite pandemic pastimes. It felt luxurious and leisurely, especially in those blissfully warm spring and fall afternoons.

I began reading more extensively again, something I had struggled to do since becoming a parent. I've always loved reading, but for that first decade of motherhood, it felt nearly impossible to fit in before the end of the day... and by then, I was usually asleep before I turned the page. Rediscovering that joy felt like reconnecting with an old part of myself I didn't realize I'd missed.

THE MIRROR OF NEURODIVERGENCE

My sister told me once, "You're always working on yourself. A lot of people don't do that, but it's something I see you doing—and I'm proud of you for it."

She was right. Especially during COVID, especially in sobriety, I turned inward. While the world busied itself with home renovation projects, I focused on renovating myself, becoming better for my kids, my husband, my team, and most of all, for me. How I showed up mattered, and I took that responsibility seriously...I take most things seriously.

Around that same time, I began to see myself more clearly through the mirror of neurodivergence, a word that refers to people whose brains work differently than what's considered typical. I'll share more about that journey later, but in those early days, all I knew was that the way I processed, felt, and responded to the world wasn't wrong, it was just different. And it deserved understanding.

That looked like slowing down and listening more, especially to myself. I started taking more long walks and hikes, giving my thoughts space to breathe. I spent hours on my deck couch and hammock reading more than thirty books that year, from moving memoirs to practical wisdom, from soul-deep reflections to laugh-out-loud storytelling.

I devoured works like "Becoming" by Michelle Obama, "Dare to Lead" and "Daring Greatly" by Brené Brown, "Untamed" and "Love Warrior" by Glennon Doyle, "Educated" by Tara Westover, "I'm Still Here" by Austin Channing Brown, "Braiding Sweetgrass" by Robin Wall Kimmerer, and "Dear Girls" by Ali Wong. Looking back, I didn't realize at the time that I was being quietly mentored by a chorus of alcohol-free women: Elizabeth Gilbert, Glennon, Brené. They were further down the path, and they spoke to parts of me I was still rediscovering.

I also read books like "The Hate U Give"and "The Subtle Art of Not Giving a F*ck," not because I needed a new worldview, but because they affirmed what I already believed and strengthened it. I went to a middle school where nearly half the student body was Black, and that experience shaped how I saw the world. It gave me a sense of cultural awareness and equity that had been part of me for a long time. These books didn't open my eyes, they gave me language for things I'd already seen and felt.

They reiterated why it's important to keep paying attention. To keep listening, learning, advocating, and showing up, even when it's uncomfortable. Especially then.

They reminded me that with my privilege came responsibility, not just to be aware, but to take meaningful action. To use my voice, my platform, and my position in ways that supported and lifted others, especially those whose voices had too often been ignored or silenced. Privilege wasn't something to hold passively, it was a responsibility to put to work. To show up, to speak up, and to make space in ways that truly supported equity and the greater good... for all.

This chapter of my life wasn't about becoming someone new. It was about peeling back the noise, the fear, the pressure and becoming more me than I'd ever allowed myself to be.

Incorporating more play and joy is something I'm still working on. I think it's part trauma response, part firstborn energy. Being neurodivergent only added to the complexity: not catching social cues, missing the punchline, being perceived as intense or serious because I was often deep in thought or laser-focused on a task.

Throughout school and in many of my jobs, I'd hear things like, "You should smile more," or "Are you upset?" I used to have a shelter manager who'd gently remind me to "check your face" before walking into the shelter.

I can laugh about it now, but being intentionally aware of your facial expressions (especially when you aren't wired to smile or default to relaxed features) can be exhausting.

But I listened, because it mattered. In shelter, and at home.

So if you ever catch me with a look that seems a little off... it's a work in progress. And I'm giving myself more permission to be human. Permission to be me.

Maybe this is where the term resting bitch face came from. We're not mad, we're just managing fifty tabs in our mental browser while trying to remember if we thawed the chicken. Honestly, resting bitch face might just be what quietly carrying the mental load looks like. Prioritizing facial expressions is pretty far down the list when you're doing the job of three people.

Instead of policing each other's expressions, maybe we start talking about and sharing the weight. The load gets lighter when we carry it together.

THE NEW LENS

Throughout this time of a slow returning to myself, my therapist gently reminded me I was supposed to be spending more time resting and less time producing. This was a radical shift for someone like me. Probably for most of us. She even joked that I needed to read something other than personal or professional development.

But it worked.

I had slowly brought myself into a more regulated state, and life was finally hitting differently.

It was in the second half of my fourth alcohol-free year that I began studying neurodiversity more deeply. I hadn't realized it at the time, but it had become my new special interest. I was reading "Divergent Mind: Thriving in a World That Wasn't Designed for You" by Jenara Nerenberg, hoping to understand myself and my children more fully.

I already knew I was a Highly Sensitive Person (HSP) and had sensory processing disorder—traits that became glaringly obvious in the early days of living alcohol free and shelter work. I had learned more about sensory differences by parenting my kids through their own experiences with clothing discomfort, food textures, and environmental overstimulation. Suddenly, things I had always struggled with made so much more sense.

Nerenberg's work opened a new window of understanding:

"When it comes to women, sensory processing differences are often overlooked, masked, or mistaken for something else entirely. Between a flawed system that focuses on diagnosing younger, male populations, and the fact that girls are conditioned from a young age to blend in and conform to gender expectations, women often don't learn about their neurological differences until they are adults, if at all. As a result, potentially millions live with undiagnosed or misdiagnosed neurodivergences, and the misidentification leads to depression, anxiety, low self-esteem, and shame. Meanwhile, we all miss out on the gifts their neurodivergent minds have to offer."

Reading that felt like being seen...for the first time, in full light.

10

THE SPACE BETWEEN PANIC & PEACE
THE FRIDAY THAT FLATTENED ME

ONE FRIDAY, I was feeling especially rundown and left work a little early. It had been a long work week, following a long weekend trip to New York City for winter break. Between travel recovery, field hockey, a work dinner, and prepping to celebrate the kids' birthdays with family the next day, I was wiped out.

I got home early and planned to lie down before taking Parker to the school dance that evening. Matt had just made a snack and walked upstairs to his office to wrap up a few things. He was going to grab Parker from the bus stop so I could rest for a bit.

I was in the kitchen filling my water cup when I heard it, that all-too-familiar cry for help. It's a specific sound Matt makes when a seizure begins. I froze for half a second, listening. Then my body jolted into action. I grabbed the magnet off the refrigerator and sprinted upstairs.

His hands were bent up toward his forearms in that crooked position I've come to recognize. I'm not sure why it happens, but it's common during his seizures. He sometimes complains of wrist pain afterward, and I tell him it's probably from the awkward posture his body locks into during these episodes.

This time, panic hit me hard. He had likely fallen into the wall and slid down, headfirst. His body was stiff and jerking violently. Moving him is always difficult, but now I had to be extra careful. The angle of his neck terrified me, if he jerked too hard or I moved him wrong, he could be seriously injured. I knew I had to swipe him with a magnet first, to stimulate his VNS.

I knelt beside him and gently wrapped my right hand around his head and neck to support him. His face had turned blue. His eyes were rolled back. His mouth opened and closed in gasping motions: an extreme, open-mouthed frown that always feels like watching death move across his face. It's unbearable. Time slows. He looks as if he's dying.

I whispered, "Breathe."

And he did. Not because he heard me, he isn't present when it happens. But somehow, maybe on some deep level, he took a breath. I don't know how. I just know I was grateful.

He had been eating BBQ chips before the seizure, so while watching his body convulse, I also scanned for any sign of a blocked airway. There was red and orange on the carpet and dripping from the side of his mouth. Was it blood or just seasoning? At first glance, it looked like paprika, maybe oil from the chips. I saw no visible injuries, but I stayed alert for anything hidden inside his mouth.

With my left hand, I swiped the magnet across the VNS, his vagus nerve stimulation device, implanted in his chest. I waited for the signal to help soften his body. If I could get him to release even slightly, I could reposition him without causing more harm.

At the same time, I used my voice: "Siri, call Matt's dad."

My hands were full, but I needed help, someone had to get to the bus stop. My voice shook as I spoke into my watch, "I need you to pick him up at the bus stop," I pleaded, breathless and desperate. I couldn't remember the last time I felt so frantic.

He heard it immediately in my tone. "Matthew?" he asked.

"Yes," I said. "I'm with him. I think he's okay, but someone needs to get Parker."

"I've got him," he said without hesitation.

By then, Matt's convulsing had slowed. His chest started rising more steadily. Color returned to his face, bit by bit. Then came the gasps... those deep, primal pulls of oxygen that fill his lungs after they've been deprived. His head tilted back, his mouth opened, and his body tried to catch up. It's always one of the hardest parts to witness, those first ragged breaths, his system fighting its way back.

This time, he regained mobility more quickly than usual. He halfway returned to the room, his eyes darting around, his head trying to make sense of where he was and what had happened. "It's okay," I said gently, trying to calm him as he floated between confusion and awareness.

I always wonder what it's like inside his brain during these moments. He often wakes up in what seems like a panic, his eyes unfocused and searching. It reminds me of waking from a nightmare —the kind where you've been running from something terrifying, heart pounding, cortisol coursing through your veins. To me, his eyes always ask the same questions: What happened? Am I safe? Am I okay?

"It's okay," I repeat. "You're okay."

I touch his face and smile softly.

"I love you," he says. And my heart sinks.

Because I'll never fully know what he experiences in those moments. Some of it may disappear with the fog, while other parts might be too painful to name. I stay calm for him. To help regulate his nervous system. But in doing so, I feel the energy drain from my own. Like I'm lending him my grounding, giving him what I've got left.

It takes everything out of me.

Luckily, Grandpa was already scheduled to pick up Olivia that day, so I had more space to manage what was unfolding at home. I followed up 20 minutes later to say Matt was okay, then asked if he could pick up dinner. He agreed, and I sent him our order. I don't know how I would have gotten through the rest of the night otherwise. There were still Friday night "must-dos" ahead of us.

That is the hardest part of days when there is a seizure, life still goes on. Everyone has to eat, is the laundry ready for tomorrow, have we completed the school project, have we prepped for the next thing. Many of these are tasks that default to mothers and on these days it can feel like a blur.

And this is how life is in our house sometimes.

THE PROTECTOR-IN-WAITING

I often feel like I'm always "on." Between the unpredictability of epilepsy, being the main driver in a household with teenagers, and serving as the CEO responsible for the outcomes of every major decision at work, it's a lot. It's heavy. And while I've done a lot to stabilize our world, I carried this weight for decades without the resources or support to care for myself in the ways I truly needed.

Now, finally, my body is no longer living in the constant state of fight or flight it was trapped in for more than 30 years. Our home is calmer. Our life is more stable. But the echoes of that state still live in me, tucked into muscle memory and nervous system patterns that are hard to unwind.

I remember reading Brené Brown's "Atlas of the Heart" and feeling profoundly seen, especially in the introduction, where she described growing up with intense emotion and unpredictable behavior. She wrote:

"As the oldest, I often felt the brunt of the madness, along with the responsibility of protecting my siblings from the unpredictable swings. When things were bad, I was the protector. When things

were great, I was the protector-in-waiting, always on the outside of the fun, easily teased for being too serious, and always knowing that we were one sideways glance or one smart-ass comment away from chaos."

That. Was. Me.

As a child, I was always scanning, anticipating. Hyperaware. Managing emotions that weren't mine. Making space. Making peace. Waiting for the next shift in the atmosphere.

"For children, it's easy for everything to become a source of shame when nothing is normalized. You assume that if no one is talking about it, it must just be you."

Reading those lines cracked something open in me. They gave language to a reality I had lived but never known how to describe. They reminded me why regulation, of myself and others, had become such an instinct, and why it had also left me so exhausted.

Once my roots took hold in a life that was free from alcohol, I started to see how much I had been numbing, shrinking, over-functioning and playing small. There were years that felt terrifyingly lonely. I started looking at my surroundings differently, who and how I was spending my time and energy. Relationships started feeling different and no longer clicking. I started noticing what I required and what kind of engagements fueled me and which depleted me, sometimes leaving me on empty. There were boundaries to set, some soft, others steel-firm especially those regarding my time and access. I got really clear about my time boundaries and how accessible I made myself to others. We teach people how to treat us and I was learning to stop making other people comfortable at the expense of my own well-being.

It was the hardest work I've ever done. And it's work I continue to do.

AN ALCOHOL-FREE AWAKENING

Living alcohol-free wasn't as hard as I thought it would be. The hardest part was the loneliness and the quiet, personal grief of watching my world rearrange itself.

The truth is, COVID made it easier for me to stop drinking. While so much of the world leaned into day drinking, Zoom happy hours, and alcohol delivery services, I was quietly pulling myself out of that current. It was oddly helpful: the distance, the quiet, the pause. But it was also incredibly isolating.

I started building a new support system, slowly and intentionally. Although AA has helped many people and continues to be a lifeline for others, it wasn't the right fit for me. The structure felt like it was built for someone else's journey. As a neurodivergent woman, the intensity of the rooms—the big energies, the raw recoveries, the emotional openness—often overwhelmed my nervous system. Those early days were exhausting. I needed something calmer. More contained. More sustainable.

I heard messages like, "If you're not consistent with meetings, you're not committed," but I was committed—to healing in a way that honored all of me. Honestly, it was just too much for me to show up multiple times a week. I needed something quieter. More grounded. More flexible.

And I didn't want to lead with a label. "Hi, I'm Amy, and I'm an alcoholic," never felt like the whole truth. Because I'm not defined by what I've quit. I'm defined by what I've chosen.

So I took to nature, the way I always have when I need to think, to heal, to breathe. Trees don't ask questions. Trails don't talk over you. The stillness welcomed me, reminded me who I was, and gave me the space to reclaim my peace.

I've chosen clarity. I've chosen presence. I've chosen a life where I no longer need to numb or hide. That's the commitment I've made. I'm a visionary. A leader. An artist. A neurodivergent mother. A strategic thinker. A trauma survivor. A woman with silver hair and a fire in her chest.

I'm not fundamentally broken... I just needed new tools.

I'm in recovery from emotional neglect, childhood chaos, people pleasing, perfectionism, codependency, and grief. I survived being a child in the '80s, when we actually had public service announcements reminding parents to look for their kids. Still, I lost my parents too early. I wholeheartedly believe they were doing the best they could with what they had. They, too, were likely parenting from a place they weren't given. In their day children were to be seen, not heard. I think once they started hearing us, they weren't quite sure what to do, so they often sent us outdoors... for the whole day.

I masked my neurodivergence for decades. I use this broad term used to describe people whose brains work differently from what's considered "typical." Whether in how they think, feel, learn, or process the world around them. It's not something to be fixed; it's simply a different way of being. I was a gifted child who learned to survive by shrinking, pleasing, and staying quiet. The unspoken rules were clear: Don't talk about family matters. Don't ask too many questions about personal business. Don't take up too much space.

And don't need too much. That was the script I inherited. Don't question what the adults are doing...just do it because they said so.

Because if we needed too much or became too much, they would need something to take the edge off, something to cope. This "something" usually came with rippling consequences for everyone in the household , and you never knew of what caliber. But those were the times, that's what so many people did. That was my lineage. And I also inherited so much strength.

As for the wisdom of my ancestors, those were my gifts too, they taught me to be peaceful and stand up for what I believed in and I sure better be betting on myself. Stand up for others, speak up even when my voice shakes, fight for what's right, to never throw the first punch but know how to throw one, to dream boldly, to leave every space a little better than I found it, to always find humor and beauty, to stop and pay attention to the little things and to never take shit from anyone. I miss them so much—their wisdom, and their baggage. They shaped me. And I'm healing for them, too.

Living alcohol-free gave me the space to rewrite everything— how I parent, how I lead, how I love, and how I care for myself. One day at a time, one choice at a time, I've been curating a life that reflects who I truly am. And in doing that, I've found my people—the ones who love me just as I am, who ask the hard questions, and who hold space when I need it most.

As a neurodivergent woman, safe relationships haven't always been easy to find. I've been called too sensitive, too emotional, too much. And maybe for some, I am too much. But I've come to believe that my "too muchness" is also my power.

LEARNING TO CELEBRATE

One of the most impactful things I did for myself during this long stretch of growth was start a "Book of Wins." Somewhere in early COVID, I began writing down moments of success, both personal and professional. At first, it felt small, maybe even unnecessary. But over time, it became something I deeply treasured: a space to celebrate both quiet and bold victories, and a reminder of the magic that can unfold with persistent grit and determination.

That book helped me track the real journey, not just the milestones, but the resilience behind them.

It captured the big leaps and the tiniest wins: expanding programming, securing new funding, opening shelter doors wider, building better systems, and supporting a team on the edge of burnout. It also held space for the deeply personal triumphs—like choosing an alcohol-free life and sticking with it through loneliness, grief, and reinvention. It marked my first alcohol-free holidays, the conferences I braved solo, and the trips that reconnected me to myself in ways I never expected.

It honored the days I showed up, for myself, for my family, for my team, for the women we served, especially on days when I felt like I had nothing left to give.

I still turn to it in heavier moments, flipping back through the pages to remember how far I've come. Everyone should have a Book of Wins because we are all carrying more than the world sees, and we all deserve to honor the work we're doing, one step at a time.

As women, we rarely pause long enough to acknowledge our own progress. We power through, keep going, handle the next crisis, check the next box. We don't transition well from one win to the next because we're too busy doing. We rarely reflect, let alone celebrate. A practice that often comes with the price of our health and wellness.

So in my forties, I started making celebration a practice, both at home and at work. I brought it into my parenting, into my marriage, into my leadership. I celebrated team milestones and personal milestones. I reminded myself that joy is just as worthy of attention as hardship.

At work, we celebrated navigating seasons of growth with grace and feeling supported, individual successes of our clients, their getting keys and getting housed or getting certain documentation that had taken months that eliminated a barrier to their housing. We celebrated team members graduating college or MSW programs and their next chapters. We make it a goal to find something to celebrate at the end of every shift.

We'd made it through the trenches of COVID. We'd served thousands of women. We'd kept showing up, kept offering a safe space, kept evolving, even as the world felt like it was falling apart. Our organization didn't just survive; it grew. It flourished. And I did, too.

At home, we celebrate. Birthdays and anniversaries, another year since Matt and I met, another year alcohol free, doing hard things, pushing ourselves out of our comfort zones, planning adventurous trips. Even Fridays, with a movie, pizza, and ice cream sundae spread. Trying to play up the little things and finding reasons to celebrate can be so powerful.

This journey cracked me open. It pulled me to my knees. It forced me to face the trauma I hadn't processed, the wounds I hadn't touched. It whispered that it was time to stop coping and start healing. And as hard as it was, it pushed me forward into the next version of myself.

THE BAG THAT CHANGED
EVERYTHING

In my third year alcohol-free, something shifted.

Samantha began volunteering at the shelter, a woman I didn't know well at first. Months later, while interviewing her for a shelter manager role, I realized she had a son the same age as mine. And she was also alcohol-free and had written a book about it and done a TedX talk.

Samantha introduced me to a small group of women who called themselves the "Fun Killers." It was perfect. They had started meeting weekly the year before and slowly added members—moms who had grown tired of the constant drinking culture around kids' activities, PTA meetings, even on the sidelines at swim meets. The group became a sanctuary. We shared frustrations, resources, laughter, and hard stories—about partners, parents, shame, recovery, and freedom. We exchanged book recommendations, celebrated milestones, and gave each other permission to show up fully, unapologetically.

That group filled a hole I hadn't known how to name in a season that required more support. It was one example of the kind of community I'd been craving for years, a place where I didn't have to explain myself, where I could exhale.

By year four, I was ready for something more. I signed up—nervously—for a woman's conference in Chicago. It felt indulgent, even selfish, to plan a solo trip. But something inside me said go. When I saw Elizabeth Gilbert was the keynote speaker, I was all in. Her book "Big Magic" had become a winter ritual for me, a creative recharge and the fact that she was also alcohol-free made it feel meant to be.

So I booked the trip, the room, the flight. I listened to that small voice inside me that was learning to trust again.

That weekend changed everything. I met incredible women who became part of my ongoing support circle. I found a weekly dance class. I joined a weekly mom group call. I expanded my network in ways that nourished me deeply. These women didn't just see me, they celebrated me. We laughed together, cried together, shared hard things that only neurodivergent mothers can understand. About ourselves, our relationships, parenting, and children. We grew together, cried together. We shared the heartbreakingly hard moments and we cheered each other on for the wins.

And then, on a sunny afternoon, during that trip to Chicago, I walked into a Louis Vuitton store.

I'd wanted one of their bags since the seventh grade but had always told myself no. Too expensive. Too lavish. Too much. But as I stood there, something shifted. How could I not?

It cost less than a year of alcohol and self-sabotage.

I hesitated. My daughter and husband encouraged me—twice—to go back and get it. So I did. And as I stepped out onto Michigan Avenue with my new bag in hand, head high, shoulders back, sun on my face, I felt electric.

It wasn't about the bag. It was about what it represented—worth, joy, permission. That purchase woke something up in me. A new level of confidence. A deeper connection to my highest self.

Within three months, I was mapping out my succession plan. I was dreaming about a new level of advocacy, new business—consulting, coaching, writing. I joined my friend Samantha's writing group and started the memoir my friends had been telling me I should write since I was a teenager. I had moved my body out of a constant state of flight-or-flight for the first time probably in my life.

The bag wasn't just a reward. It was a declaration—I'm done shrinking.

Because I can have a servant's heart *and* a designer handbag.

11

THE RETURN TO MYSELF
SOUTH OF THE CIRCLE, CLOSE TO THE LIGHT

IN THE MONTHS THAT FOLLOWED, something deeper began to settle. I noticed I was breathing differently. Walking differently. I was no longer moving through life in a constant state of vigilance. For the first time—maybe ever—I felt grounded. Present. Safe in my own body.

That's when I really began to embrace my neurodivergence.

It wasn't a label, it was a homecoming. A framework. A mirror that helped me understand my sensory experiences, my social exhaustion, my hyper-empathy, my pattern recognition. It explained why relationships had always felt both sacred and overwhelming, why I'd often been misread, and why I sometimes misread others. It helped me see myself not as broken but as wired differently, exquisitely.

It was like closing the loop on a lifetime of wondering: Why does this feel harder for me than it does for other people? The answer wasn't that I was failing. The answer was that I was masking. For years. Decades.

I came full circle, only this time, I was coming as the healed version of myself.

That healing included grief. Letting go of people who no longer fit. Accepting that some relationships were meant for a different version of me, the one who stayed quiet, made herself small, didn't make trouble, didn't ask for too much, let her boundaries be trampled over. As I expanded, some connections naturally fell away. Not out of anger, but from truth. From alignment. From growth.

And it hurt. But it also freed me.

Today, I take action sooner. I overthink less. I trust myself more. I'm learning to enjoy my creative momentum, even when I have to remind myself not to launch too many ships at once.

Years ago, I stood at the base of a Grinnell glacier in Montana, watching others climb it, aching to join, to finish. We'd hit ice and my kids were already ready to turn back. And I wasn't equipped to reach the glacier, not then. I didn't have the crampons. The tools.

And then, in Iceland, I did.

It was a once-in-a-lifetime trip with my daughter, sixteen, radiant, and on the cusp of adulthood. I knew we were lucky. I knew we wouldn't always travel like this, just the two of us. She'd go on and embark on her own journeys in life. And so I said yes. To the flight. To the three layers of clothing. To the stillness I'd forgotten how much I needed.

For the first time in a long time, I was carried. No decisions to make. No one needing me. Just the rhythm of the itinerary, the hum of our cozy bus, and the fierce Icelandic winds pressing into my coat. I was allowed to simply follow. To rest. And in that rest, something stirred.

Each day brought movement, black sand beaches, volcanic plains, geysers, glacial blue waters, wild horses, a glacier climb. And then, on the final day, a last minute hike—Mount Esja. This one hadn't been on the itinerary but was a group decision to embark on. Not everyone understood what we were taking on but I did. I quickly searched it on my All Trails app and learned what we had in store, over 2,000 feet of elevation in under two hours. A sharp, steep climb. At times, I was scaling the side of the mountain on all fours, without the proper equipment, fully questioning my life choices.

But I kept going.

We climbed into the snow capped mountain, the wind picked up and it became increasingly bright. As I reached the top, the snow blanketed the rocks, and the wind whipped through the stillness. To my right, the sea. To my left, the vast, rugged beauty of Iceland. The sky opened. The light, the beauty and the view broke through. I was just south of the Arctic Circle, filled with pride. Beaming, I felt breathless—in every way that matters. Fully alive. Small and strong at once. It was there, in the stillness above the clouds, that I realized: I had come back to myself.

I was completely reinvigorated. I remembered what it felt like to be ignited. To be moved by nature. To feel wonder—not as something fleeting, but as something returned.

Living alcohol-free gave me clarity. But healing gave me light.

For so long, it felt like I was living in the shadows, coping, striving, surviving. Like I was standing in the path of an eclipse, unsure if the light would ever return.

But it did. Slowly, then all at once.

AND IN THAT LIGHT, I finally saw myself clearly, not perfect, not invincible—but whole.

I wasn't just becoming myself.

I was myself.

Fully. Finally.

And the light had broken through.

AFTERWORD

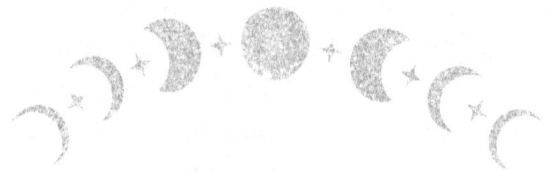

Sometime in the quiet middle stretch of writing this book, when I found myself waking earlier and earlier, as if someone—or something—was nudging me toward the page.

As I continued writing, my ancestors began appearing, guiding me, cheering me on, reminding me they were here. I had buried so much for so long that their voices had grown faint. When you're numb to pain, you're also numb to joy, to your own inner voice, intuition and spirituality. Healing was what let me hear them again. It cleared the fog and reconnected me to my light and to theirs.

"Got any big deals cookin'?" I hear TW ask, and then I wake up. It's 4:00 a.m. I smile and feel his presence. It's one week away from the three-year anniversary of his death and, as a matter of fact, I do have some big deals cooking.

Even though it's early and I'd rather stay in bed, I push myself to get up, to write and see what comes to me in the magical window of these early morning hours when inspiration so often hits me.

I put on my slippers and robe, make a cup of coffee, and shuffle into the dining room—my makeshift office—to begin writing my morning pages.

A few weeks later, I dreamt of my Nanny. We were in a beautiful landscape that seemed like a backyard garden with a long and winding pathway.

She smiled big and bright, genuinely delighted to see me, and asked, "Want to go for a walk?"

We strolled through the heavenly landscape.

I could feel them drawing nearer, my parents too. Although my parents seemed further away, they were still on the distant horizon. They kept emerging, just before I drifted off to sleep, first thing in the morning, alongside me on my hikes. I felt their collective presence guiding me, cheering me on, reminding me they were still with me.

I had buried so much for so long that I'd lost sight of my own inner light. My connection to life. My voice. My ability to hear what's been trying to speak to me all along.

Healing changed that. It brought clarity. It reconnected me to myself—and to them.

That morning, with the taste of coffee on my tongue and my slippers soft against the floor, I felt them with me, my grandfather asking about "big deals cooking," my grandmother smiling from her wheelchair, and sometimes standing, waving from no wheelchair at all. Their presence reminded me of where I come from and made me wonder what I might be walking toward next.

Some paths we walk alone. Some we walk with those who came before us. Either way, they light the way.

THE MIXED TAPE

1. As — Stevie Wonder
2. Into the Groove — Madonna
3. All She Wants to Do Is Dance — Don Henley
4. Billie Jean — Michael Jackson
5. Material Girl — Madonna
6. Sgt. Pepper's Lonely Hearts Club Band—The Beatles
7. Pink Floyd—Time
8. Home Sweet Home — Mötley Crüe
9. (I've Had) The Time of My Life — Bill Medley, Jennifer Warnes
10. Girls Just Want to Have Fun — Cyndi Lauper
11. At Last — Etta James
12. Days Like This — Van Morrison
13. Life Uncommon — Jewel
14. Down So Long — Jewel
15. Name — The Goo Goo Dolls
16. I Hope You Dance — LeeAnn Womack
17. Amie — Pure Prairie League
18. Melissa — The Allman Brothers Band
19. Canon in D Major — Johann Pachelbel, String Quartet

20. Universe & U — KT Tunstall

21. Feist — Musha Boom

22. Keep Breathing — Ingrid Michaelson

23. Time of the Season—The Zombies

24. Johnny Cash—Ring of Fire

25. Unstoppable — Sia

26. Hands — Jewel

27. Signed, Sealed, Delivered (I'm Yours) — Stevie Wonder

RESOURCES

Books

Brown, A.C. (2018). *I'm still here: Black dignity in a world made for whiteness.* Convergent Books. HarperCollins+12YouTube+12Wikipedia+12

Brown, B. (2021). *Atlas of the heart: Mapping meaningful connection and the language of human experience.* Random House. WikipediaGoodreads

Brown, B.van der Kolk. (2014). *The body keeps the score: Brain, mind, and body in the healing of trauma.* Viking. (Note: year previously included by you)

Brown, B. (2018). *Dare to lead: Brave work. Tough conversations. Whole hearts.* Random House. Wikipedia+3TIME+3The New Yorker+3

Brown, B. (2012). *Daring greatly: How the courage to be vulnerable transforms the way we live, love, parent, and lead.* Avery. WikipediaPenguinRandomhouse.com

Doyle, G. (2016). *Love Warrior: A memoir.* Flatiron Books. Amazon+15Teen Vogue+15Glamour+15

Doyle, G. (2020). *Untamed*. The Dial Press. AmazonGoodreads

Kimmerer, R.W. (2013). *Braiding sweetgrass: Indigenous wisdom, scientific knowledge, and the teachings of plants*. Milkweed Editions. WikipediaMilkweed Editions

Manson, M. (2016). *The subtle art of not giving a f*ck: A counterintuitive approach to living a good life**. HarperOne. Wikipedia+11Wikipedia+11Barnes & Noble+11

Nerenberg, J. (2022). *Divergent mind: Thriving in a world that wasn't designed for you*. Morrow. (Year provided earlier)

Obama, M. (2018). *Becoming*. Crown Publishing. (Year provided earlier)

Thomas, A. (2017). *The hate u give*. Balzer + Bray. The New Yorker+12Wikipedia+12Goodreads+12

Westover, T. (2018). *Educated: A memoir*. Random House. (Year provided earlier)

Wong, A. (2019). *Dear girls: Intimate tales, untold secrets & advice for living your best life*. Random House. Amazonrandomhousebooks.com

Support Groups & Self-Help

American Cancer Society
24/7 Cancer Helpline for patients, families, and caregivers
Call: 1-800-227-2345
Website & Chat: www.cancer.org

CancerCare
Provides free support groups, counseling, and financial assistance for those affected by cancer
Call: 1-800-813-HOPE (4673)
Website: www.cancercare.org

Childhelp National Child Abuse Hotline

For children or adults needing support, reporting abuse, or healing from trauma
Call/Text: 1-800-4-A-CHILD (1-800-422-4453)
Live Chat: www.childhelp.org

Emotional Freedom Technique
Blacher, S. (2023, January 14). *Emotional Freedom Technique (EFT): Tap to relieve stress and burnout. Journal of Interprofessional Education & Practice, 30*, Article 100599. https://doi.org/10.1016/j.xjep.2023.100599 (Republished in *PubMed Central*)

Epilepsy Foundation
24/7 helpline staffed by information specialists
Phone (English): 1-800-332-1000
Phone (Español): 1-866-748-8008
Provides: guidance, referrals, and same-day follow-up on inquiries, a living with epilepsy section, great for preparedness and creating an action plan, support for parents and caregivers
(National Office)
General inquiries and national assistance
Phone: 301-459-3700

Grounding Techniques
Johns Hopkins University Human Resources, and Johns Hopkins Employee Assistance Program (JHEAP). (n.d.). *Grounding techniques to help control anxiety* [PDF]. Retrieved August 12, 2025, from https://hr.jhu.edu/wp-content/uploads/JHEAP-Grounding-Techniques-to-Help-Control-Anxietypdf.pdf

National Center for Missing & Exploited Children (NCMEC)
Call: 1-800-THE-LOST (1-800-843-5678)
Website: www.missingkids.org

National Domestic Violence Hotline

For those affected by sexual violence, domestic abuse, or relationship trauma
Call: 1-800-799-SAFE (7233)
Text: "START" to 88788
Chat: www.thehotline.org

RAINN (Rape, Abuse & Incest National Network)
24/7 National Sexual Assault Hotline
Call: 1-800-656-HOPE (4673)
Online Chat: www.rainn.org

Self Help for Trauma App
Peaceful Heart Network. (2025, August 9). *Self Help for Trauma* (Version 1.9.0) [Mobile app description]. Apple App Store. Retrieved August 12, 2025, from https://apps.apple.com/us/app/self-help-for-trauma/id1394291317

Tapping
The Tapping Solution Foundation. (n.d.). *The Tapping Solution Foundation.* Retrieved August 12, 2025, from https://www.tappingsolutionfoundation.org/

MEDIA CREDITS

Bill Medley & Jennifer Warnes. (1987). *[I've had] The time of my life* [Recorded by Bill Medley & Jennifer Warnes]. On *Dirty dancing* [Soundtrack]. RCA.

Cash, J. (1963). *Ring of fire* [Song]. On *Ring of Fire: The Best of Johnny Cash*. Columbia Records.

Craven, W. (Director). (1984). *A nightmare on Elm Street* [Film]. New Line Cinema.

Don Henley. (1985). *All she wants to do is dance* [Recorded by Don Henley]. On *Building the perfect beast* [Album]. Geffen.

Pure Prairie League. (1972). *Amie* [Recorded by Pure Prairie League]. On *Bustin' out* [Album]. RCA.

Stevie Wonder. (1976). *As* [Recorded by Stevie Wonder]. On *Songs in the key of life* [Album]. Motown.

Etta James. (1960). *At last* [Recorded by Etta James]. On *At last* [Album]. Argo.

Michael Jackson. (1985). *Billie Jean* [Recorded by Michael Jackson]. On *Thriller* [Album]. Epic.

Pachelbel, J. (1680). *Canon in D* [Composition].

Van Morrison. (1995). *Days like this* [Recorded by Van Morrison]. On *Days like this* [Album]. Polydor.

Jewel. (1991). *Down so long* [Recorded by Jewel]. On *Spirit* [Album]. Atlantic.

Lauper, C. (1983). *Girls just wanna have fun* [Recorded by Cyndi Lauper]. On *She's so unusual* [Album]. Portrait.

Ardolino, E. (Director). (1987). *Dirty dancing* [Film]. Vestron Pictures.

Hooper, T. (Director). (1974). *The Texas chain saw massacre* [Film]. Bryanston Distributing Company.

Mötley Crüe. (1985). *Home sweet home* [Recorded by Mötley Crüe]. On *Theatre of pain* [Album]. Elektra.

Ingrid Michaelson. (2007). *Keep breathing* [Recorded by Ingrid Michaelson]. On *Be OK* [Album]. Cabin 24.

Jewel. (1991). *Life uncommon* [Recorded by Jewel]. On *Spirit* [Album]. Atlantic.

Madonna. (1984). *Like a virgin* [Recorded by Madonna]. On *Like a virgin* [Album]. Sire.

Madonna. (1984). *Material girl* [Recorded by Madonna]. On *Like a virgin* [Album]. Sire.

The Allman Brothers. (1972). *Melissa* [Recorded by The Allman Brothers]. On *Eat a peach* [Album]. Capricorn.

Feist. (2004). *Mushaboom* [Recorded by Feist]. On *Let it die* [Album]. Arts & Crafts.

Goo Goo Dolls. (1995). *Name* [Recorded by Goo Goo Dolls]. On *A boy named Goo* [Album]. Warner Bros.

O'Connor, S. (1990). *Nothing compares 2 U* [Recorded by Sinéad O'Connor]. On *I do not want what I haven't got* [Album]. Chrysalis. (Originally written by Prince, 1984).

Forman, M. (Director). (1988). *Rain man* [Film]. United Artists.

The Zombies. (1968). *Time of the season* [Recorded by The Zombies]. On *Odessey and oracle* [Album]. CBS.

Madonna. (1985). *Into the groove* [Recorded by Madonna]. On *Desperately seeking Susan original soundtrack* [Soundtrack]. Sire.

Stevie Wonder. (1970). *Signed, sealed, delivered (I'm yours)* [Recorded by Stevie Wonder]. On *Signed, sealed, delivered* [Album]. Tamla.

The Beatles. (1967). *Sgt. Pepper's Lonely Hearts Club Band* [Recorded by The Beatles]. On *Sgt. Pepper's Lonely Hearts Club Band* [Album]. Parlophone.

KT Tunstall. (2004). *Universe & U* [Recorded by KT Tunstall]. On *Eye to the telescope* [Album]. Relentless.

Fleming, V. (Director). (1939). *The wizard of Oz* [Film]. Metro-Goldwyn-Mayer.

Womack, L. (2000). I hope you dance [Recorded by Lee Ann Womack]. On *I hope you dance* [Album]. MCA Nashville.

ACKNOWLEDGMENTS

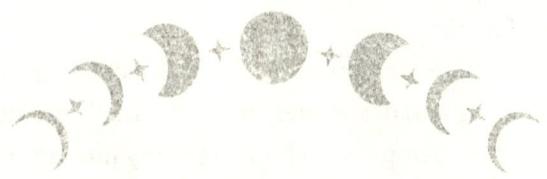

This book has been a lifetime in the making. I distinctly remember riding around in the car one night with some girlfriends in college. We were chatting about life and I remember one of them telling me, "You should write a book." I felt the goosebumps in my body and I knew I was supposed to pay attention. And I've held the idea close ever since.

I have thought of that moment often over the last few years, I can hear the words and feel myself in the car. I've always loved to write and journaling has helped me process many of the hardest moments of my life. I could feel inspiration and intuition nudging me towards the page these last few years and I knew it was time.

My family has been incredibly supportive as I hyper-focused on mornings, evenings, and weekends to bring the book to fruition. This process has cracked me open and made me whole. I am forever grateful to Matt, Olivia, and Parker for their support, patience, encouragement and understanding, it has meant the world to me.

I am forever grateful for those who inspired me, supported me, held space for me, encouraged me and listened to me as I flushed out some of the most tender and delicate pieces of my life. What an honor this journey has been.

To each of you who played a role in my story—whether named here or not—your imprint on my life is deeply felt and I carry it with gratitude and grace.

* * *

Olivia, words can't possibly describe what an incredibly bright light and source of inspiration you have been. You've taught me to reach higher, dream bigger and ask better questions. I hope you'll be my travel partner for life!

Parker, you are my North Star. You inspire and challenge me in ways I never saw coming and desperately needed. Thank you for showing me a mirror and for being such a blessing in my life. I hope we can always spend time in nature together.

Matt, thank you for your grace and blessing in allowing me to share such intimate details of our journey. Thank you for loving me fiercely, exactly as I am. Thank you for the patience, space and encouragement that lets me dream big —from adventurous vacations to starting businesses. You are an incredibly steady, funny, kind, and brilliant light in my life. The fates took my parents too soon, and then they gifted me you. I'm forever grateful.

Darrell, thank you for sharing your incredible music collection— even sometimes unknowingly. Thanks for always giving a damn, for teaching me I don't have to take shit off of anyone and the long drives to the middle of nowhere for no reason other than to be together and share good music. Your patience and kind, gentle spirit were some of the greatest blessings of my childhood. Thank you for making it so memorable, loud clocks and all!

Cher, thank you for instilling in me a fierce sense of independence, for always making sure I knew I had options and pushing me towards my best life. I'm sorry I've been blocked for so long. Writing this story cracked me open, healed me and made me whole and I'm finding my way back to you. I've got lots of big things on the horizon, I can't wait for you to see.

TW, thank you for the endless opportunities, a magical farm to experience nature and my childhood, my entrepreneurial experience, more laughter, support and love than I could have ever hoped for. Thanks for being such a bright spot and safe place.

Iris, thank you for always filling me with love and light, your sweet angelic spirit still sings to me. I'll always treasure our time together. I appreciate you always making sure the holidays were celebrated and the ordinary days were filled with laughter.

Sabrina, I'm sorry I didn't fight harder for you. I was still a kid too, lost and trying to find my way. Our journey has been a complex one. I hope in this season that we find our way to connection, community, and laughter in safe spaces. All I wanted was to be close to you in that way. You were the coolest riding that horse around with such a creative flair.

Claire, I'm sorry for the years I was less present, when I took a break to tend to my own roots and growth. It was never personal, I always adored you and our time together. I loved when I got to be your fun big sister too, those were the best days riding around in the Miata. I'm so proud of the woman you have become. I'm so blessed to call you my sister and love to watch you bloom in your own season of motherhood.

Sonny, I'm more grateful for you and your influence than you will ever know. Thank you for all you gave to bring happiness, joy and humor to TW, the farm and our family. You're a gem.

Les, I was beyond blessed to have you in my life. Thank you for all that you gave to mom, to me and my sisters. You left such a unique and impactful mark on our lives and brought joy and laughter to our days. Thank you for all the sacrifices you made to help our family.

Samantha, I'm so thankful the fates brought us together—first as sober support, and then as a partner in bringing this book, a lifetime in the making, into the world. Your endless support, countless hours of editing, and steady encouragement have been a gift beyond measure. I can't wait to see how we team up next.

Becky, I really enjoyed our time together. I am so grateful we got to work together on this book. Thank you for witnessing my story, encouraging me to dig deeper and helping me to tell it in its most powerful version.

Vitale, words can't truly express how grateful I am for all the ways you've helped me grow. From coaching, to sobriety support, to evolving friendship, you cheered me on as I crossed the finish line and kept reaching for my dreams. Your presence has been a steady light on my path.

Talley, I'm so delighted we reconnected after meeting so many years ago in middle school. Here's to sparking change, big dreams and making the world a better place than we found it!

Cheryl, thank you for walking me through the early days living an alcohol-free life. It was such unfamiliar territory in already unprecedented times, your willingness to take my texts and calls—always—meant more than I can say. I'm honored to call you my friend.

Charley and Judy, words can't truly express how grateful I am for all the ways you've supported our family—from helping with the kids to answering emergency calls, and believing in me and offering support as we launched UP. Your care has been a cornerstone of this journey, and I'm so thankful.

Andrea, my co-founder, whose insight and persistence were key in founding UP. You recognized a gap in care for women and brought that vision forward, and together we turned an idea into a reality. The roots we planted in those early days remain part of the strength of UP's story. I am grateful for the vision we shared, the beautiful story UP's founding became, and the foundation we built together.

To UP's Board Members, thank you for going above and beyond in your service. In the early days, your mentorship and steady guidance helped me gain my footing and offered an invaluable sounding board. Your presence and leadership have shaped UP into the incredible organization it is today—one that has served thousands of women with dignity and care.

To the early UP team, Shannon, Shannon, Joy, Ana, thank you for your grace and patience as I found my footing in those early years of leadership. You navigated the growing pains with me, embraced the vision, and helped bring UP from its first steps into a thriving organization. Your dedication and belief in the mission have left an indelible mark on both my life and this story.

To the 2025 UP leadership, Bailey, Dawn, Deanna, Julie and Ryan, thank you for the heart, energy, and compassion you bring to the work we do. It has been my honor to work alongside you. I'm grateful for your patience and grace as I test limits, explore bold ideas, and challenge us to think and grow creatively. The ride isn't always smooth, but look how far we've come—thanks to you.

For every UP guest who trusted me with her story, who showed me what courage looks like in its rawest and truest form, thank you for trusting UP. I hope you are safe and finding peace.

Cecily, thank you for all the fundraising support and therapeutic calls during those COVID days. Most importantly, thank you for helping me find my way to Glacier and the Teton—that trip was pure magic. I'm grateful for our hikes, travel connection, and that UP brought us together.

To my Sunday Moms, thank you for showing up and holding space as my journey unfolded. It's been an honor to witness yours in return. What we share is sacred, and I feel so blessed to have found it.

For the Best Sellers, Samantha, Laura, and Lauren, I treasure our time together where we dove deep and got to witness each other's stories being told. Thank you for showing up on repeat so we could see it through. I can't wait to have a launch party together.

Maria, I like to tell people UP formed in your office that day we met in February 2017. Thank you for pointing us in all the right directions and for mentoring me along the way. I cherish your wisdom, all that you reflect back to me and your guidance.

Barbara, thank you for being a fierce advocate from the very beginning. From our ribbon cutting to fundraising through COVID, from singing our praises on repeat to making invaluable connections, your mentorship has been a gift I treasure.

Tammy, Talley, and Vitale, thank you for believing in me and my story. Your sponsorship made it possible to print books whose sales sent 100% of the proceeds to UP. Thank you for investing in my dreams.

My UP journey has been one of the greatest gifts and blessings of my life, one that I will treasure always—a journey that reminds me of what is possible when we press forward with fierce dedication and rebel, bad ass energy of "Who's going to stop us?"

For young Amy, who nurtured her roots until they held her steady—and for the bold, healed woman who rose from them, carrying us into the light.

"We'll fight, not out of spite
For someone must stand up for what's right
'Cause where there's a man who has no voice
There I shall go sing.
In the end, only kindness matters."
- Jewel Kilcher

ABOUT THE AUTHOR

For Amy Meredith, advocacy has never been an abstract ideal; it is the heartbeat of her life. Growing up in a free-range 1980s childhood, she learned independence early, eventually becoming the first in her family to graduate from college. But life's turning points came not only with diplomas and milestones. After losing both parents young, Amy stepped into the role of guardian to her younger sister—a responsibility that deepened her resilience, empathy, and determination to stand beside those navigating their own storms.

That same conviction carried her into the heart of Louisville, Kentucky's most vulnerable community, where she co-founded UP for Women and Children—the city's first and only day shelter for women, children, and marginalized genders experiencing homelessness. Since 2019, homelessness in Louisville has risen more than 60 percent, making the shelter an increasingly vital lifeline. As Executive Director, Amy led her team through the challenges of building a nonprofit from the ground up, sustaining services during the COVID-19 pandemic, and meeting the evolving needs of the women and families they served.

Behind these public accomplishments, a quieter, a deeply personal transformation was unfolding. In 2020, after becoming alcohol-free, Amy uncovered a truth she had long kept hidden: she was neurodivergent, carrying sensory, emotional, and social complexities she had spent decades masking. The revelation brought both reckoning and liberation, prompting her to lead, live, and heal with full authenticity.

Her journey, threaded with advocacy for epilepsy and neurodiversity, is as much about community as personal courage. Through storytelling, Amy shows that every voice matters and that stories—shared honestly—can build bridges, break stigma, and spark change.

Today, Amy continues her work in systems change with the same blend of head and heart she has carried since earning degrees in psychology and justice administration. Grounded by nature and guided by her intuition, she finds her deepest restoration outdoors. She loves planning and leading her family on adventurous vacations, often to wild, breathtaking places, returning again and again to the landscapes that remind her who she is and what matters most. She lives with her family in her hometown of Louisville and also supports fellow leaders through thoughtful advising and collaborative consulting—helping them strengthen teams, build capacity, and design trustworthy, connected, and collaborative systems that last.

You can invite Amy to speak at your event or learn more about her work helping leaders navigate succession, reinvention, and resilience. Recognized as one of Louisville's Most Admired CEOs and quoted in the Washington Post, Amy brings both credibility and candor to audiences ready to accomplish hard things without burning out.

Find out more at amymeredith.co
Email amy@amymeredith.co
Instagram @amymeredithauthor